ROSE GARRARD

ARCHIVING MY OWN HISTORY

documentation of works 1969 > 1994

Cornerhouse Manchester/South London Gallery

Contents

Rose Garrard is an influential artist. Working with Rose on the installation of the exhibition 'Between Ourselves' at Rochdale Art Gallery in 1984 proved a memorable experience. The emotional and political charge from a gallery filled with works dealing with the absence of women artists from history and the reclaiming of positive role models was very special.

During the 1980s, Rose Garrard was part of a pioneering group of women artists in Britain whose presence and practice were to shape the key cultural issues of the decade, and beyond. Like that of many of her contemporaries, Rose was searching to create new methods for the telling of new stories, invested with meanings for women and with an emphasis on communication and knowledge. Fundamental to her practice is a concern to create a socially orientated and communicative art: questioning contemporary arts relevance to society.

In the 1990s this concern has led to a shift away from the studio towards a new model of practice. Through two projects in Canada, 'Calgary Conversation', at New Art Gallery, Calgary, 1991 and 'Disclosing Dialogues' at Vancouver Art Gallery, 1992, Rose has been engaged in a series of direct exchanges, articulating relationships between herself and the gallery visitor, in the process of the making of art, live in public.

Some of the investigations initiated at Vancouver Art Gallery will continue in the 3 week live art residency 'Exchanges for Empowerment' at Cornerhouse, 22 March – 10 April 1994 and funded by the Combined Arts Unit, Arts Council of Great Britain. The link with David Thorp at South London Gallery provides a further opportunity to develop a new live work 'Arena for Conversation', 17 August – 18 September 1994, funded by London Arts Board. South London Art Gallery are co-producers of this publication; we welcome their early commitment and involvement and the consolidation it has brought to this project.

This publication provides an invaluable record of key works from 1969 > 1994. It helps preserve those works of a temporary and transient nature and works made for a specific site and context. It comes out of the recognised need for documentation of live, time based and experimental practice. And, it provides a serious acknowledgement of 25 years of practice by a professional woman artist.

As Louisa Buck points out in her introduction, in the process of archiving her own history, Rose Garrard resists a history that is fixed or static. Every piece is represented alongside the orginal commentaries that accompanied it, from a variety of sources, such as the art and popular press. The artist's voice appears as one amongst many, as one alternative in many possible readings. All the material has been selected and collated by the artist and together we would like to thank Nicola Percy for her invaluable assistance with this and both Marina Warner and John Roberts for their permission to reproduce extended extracts from their writings.

The ephemeral nature of Rose's work represents a challenge to the traditional format of the retrospective exhibition, demanding a creative approach to its presentation and interpretation. For 'Living Archives' the starting point is the debris from the orginal performances/installations re-presenting them in new configurations; to emphasise the exchanges and fluidity of ideas and meanings over time. The exhibition has been made possible with generous financial support from The Henry Moore Foundation and The Arts Council of Great Britain, to both we are indebted.

Finally, to Rose Garrard very special thanks are due, not only for the enduring commitment she has brought to the project, but for the willingness to allow us entry to the intimacies and archives of her life and work. Collaborations of this kind bring a very special privilege. The idea for the exhibition has been with us for a long time; it is a light we have kept glowing since 1988. I am delighted that the moment has finally arrived and I hope that its realisation will act as a catalyst for the creation of new works in an optimistic future.

Since the late 1960s Rose Garrard has been instrumental in exploring and engaging with ideas concerning gender, identity, status and power and the relationship between artist, model and audience; in all her work personal experiences and historical references are bound together. In an art world where success is guaged by monetary value, novelty and fashion, Garrard's practice is a conscious questioning of the primacy of this value system. However, her voice rather than being marginalised or silenced in the process eloquently retains a central and focused position.

At the nucleus of Rose Garrard's exploration is the authentic female self. The spectator feels a certain verisimilitude, a semblance or a fragment of reality in which the role of feminism as a liberating power is the consistent driving force in the making and meaning of the work. The spectator searches their own personal archives in understanding the totality and specificity of Garrard's work between private and public, language and context, subject and object, reality and myth; these are the dialogues that are disclosed.

In her Birmingham College of Art, Graduate Show of 1969, 'Boundaries' demonstrated that Garrard was already investigating the relationship of the spectator to art and was challenging the notion of art being categorised and of the spectator being at a distance or somehow separate from the work of art. 'Horizon', 1970 was considered only complete when spectators were present occupying a voyeuristic role, Garrard integrates the spectator into the work so that her art can directly touch the emotions. The spectator is not in a passive objective role but becomes the witness whose subjective feelings are engaged.

By 1977 the psychological basis of earlier sculptural work, form/perception, appearance/reality, representation/ identity have coalesced with specific auobiographical content in 'Incidents in a Garden' Acme Gallery, London. Here the use of objects, narrative and performance combine to form coherent, parallel strands of meaning.

In the 1983 'New Art' exhibition at the Tate Gallery London Garrard prized open ornate yet literal 'frames of conditioning' to suggest that the subjects, self portraits by women artists of the 15th, 16th and 17th centuries, Artemisia Gentilleschi, Judith Leyster and Elizabeth Vigée-Le Brun, can elude the confines of marginalisation, becoming visible again both as significant art and artists. During a three month residency at Birmingham City Museum & Art Gallery in 1984 Garrard examined the virtual absence of women artists, the attribution of anonymous works to male artists, and the presence of female but 'anonymous models' represented by male artists in the Museum's historical collection. Garrard's process is one of historical reclamation and self recovery. By exposing forgotten pasts she reconstructs new futures through focusing on histories, myths and memories which influenced her own conditioning as an artist and as a woman.

After a serious motorcycle accident in 1988 Garrard carried through a new commissioned work 'Out of Line' for Edge 88. Interviews with fellow patients and staff at St Bartholomews Hospital, London led to a live work and installation which explored both their and her own experience of elements which contribute to physical and psychological healing. This piece marked a new direction in her multi disciplined practice. Throughout the 1990s she has been engaged in a series of direct 'exchanges', time-based work that searches for relationships between herself and the spectator. These 'exchanges' are an attempt at bringing contemporary ethical and social issues into the gallery and the creative process is wholly dependent on participation by visitors who take an active and responsible role contributing objects, texts and images for the gallery installation.

Garrard is at the centre of a story which she is 'flowing through' and which will never finish. To a certain extent the story's theme is that there is no end and that its narrative is continuously evolving in response to conflicting or converging ideas and emotions. She offers a quiet moment, an opportunity for the spectator to create a link between the personal and the universal and to hold up a mirror to examine their own conditioning and thoughts.

At the heart of Rose Garrard's art is this sense of responsibility for the future, the power of dialogue as a way of binding people together in a world that is fragmenting before our very eyes. Her sense of equality in art, as well as in life, is an example that the consciousness of the artist in today's society is of paramount importance.

Rose Garrard is an artist whose voice never dominates but its strength is in exchanging dialogue and, in her own words is, 'Learning to listen to what's being said, not what I think I already know. A process of uncovering what I've learned not to see or hear. Creating a space for listening, for being surprised, for posssibility beyond my own prejudices and opinions.'

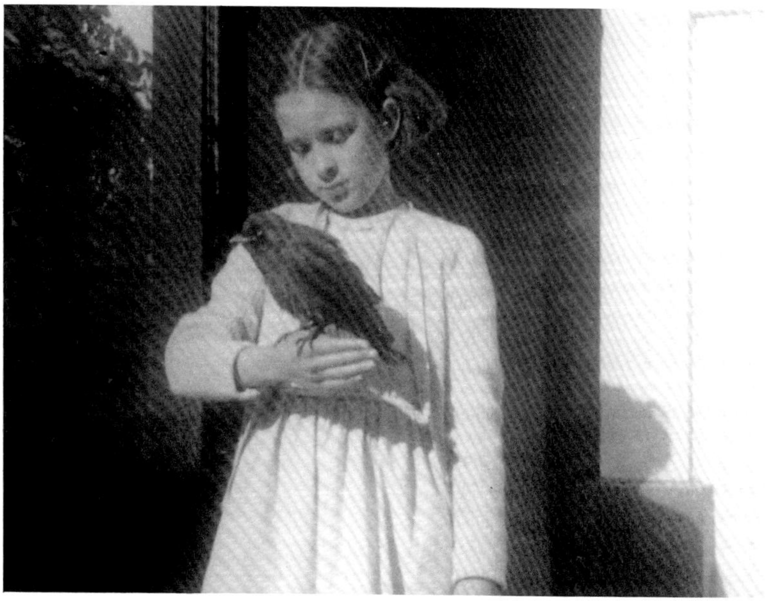

Geographers ... crowd into the edges of their maps parts of the world which they do not know about, adding notes in the margin to the effect that beyond this lies nothing but sandy deserts full of wild beasts and unapproachable bogs. (Plutarch, Life of Theseus)

In over twenty five years of interrogating the boundaries of categorisation and the absolutes of Western art history, Rose Garrard has been instrumental in mapping the shadow-lands, and proposing alternative sets of co-ordinates from which to plot a new, more authentic terrain. But, as she's the first to acknowledge, there's still a long way to go. Existing co-ordinates have to be re-examined as it becomes increasingly evident that even the areas which were widely believed to be well charted have turned out to be fraught with bias and inaccuracy; and there's an ominous contemporary parallel to the practice of ancient cartographers who used exotic marginalia to cover up unknown terrain, and in so doing only acted to make their ignorance more explicit and their hidden fears glaringly visible.

Rose Garrard is therefore faced by the problem of how to chart a career which has been spent identifying and re-negotiating existing value systems, without being forced either into a compromising conformity or banishing herself back to the margins amongst the beasts and the bogs. And just to compound the conundrum there's the additional difficulty of documenting a body of work which is not static, and wants to retain the potential for future permutations and possibilities.

Garrard's solution is to present a living alternative to the embalming process that accompanies most retrospective exhibitions. In 'Living Archives', as in all her work, she reveals that the truth, like the psyche, wears multiple facets. Just as 'Exchanges for Empowerment', her most recent piece, relies for its form and content on conversations with individuals from the different communities of Manchester, so she sets down her own history via a range of information which forces you to select your own point of view. The artist's voice appears as just one amongst many, one alternative rather than the definitive version.

In archiving two and a half decades of art production Garrard allows no hierarchy of information. She's all too aware of the way in which the actual process of historicising her work can set in motion the very value systems which she has spent the last quarter century questioning. Garrard doesn't see history as sacred and inviolate but something to be tapped into, spliced with personal experience and, whenever necessary, reclaimed and re-written. She wants a multitude of histories to co-exist simultaneously, in a way that is symbiotic but also free standing; in 'Shoemaker's Daughter' 1988 the nude tabloid pin-up is herself underpinned by the image of the Kilpeck sheelah na gig, and so today's female roles derided by the popular press can be exposed to, and empowered by their ancient and positive archetypes.

In Garrard's collation of her practice, each project appears in chronological order, but she refuses to play the art history game and define her work by category. The major works of her career – from 'Boundaries' made in 1969 when she was still a student at Birmingham College of Art, through to 'Disclosing Dialogues' produced during her residency at Vancouver Art Gallery in October 1992 – are each identified by title only, but all their components listed. Every piece is then presented with the commentaries that had originally accompanied it, whether from the popular press, art critics, or the artist herself.

In all her work Garrard weaves an elaborate web of personal and historical references, and in the same way that her own possessions become symbolic archetypes, or her own presence is simultaneously concealed and revealed, so here she presents her own terrain for excavation and interpretation. In archeology, the shard can be as precious a yielder of information as the jewel; and it's only when every strata of the site is combed for all its fragments that anything like a true picture can emerge. Like the archeologist Garrard draws on every discipline at her disposal, utilising a wide range of media and skills whilst often attaching the same weight of significance to the small personal detail as to the broad socio-political picture, and refusing to see the two as mutually exclusive.

She is all too aware, however, that in art as in life, the subject can never be fully realised, even if that subject is one of self. In the Windows series of 'Between Ourselves' 1983 Garrard puts herself as artist into each of six panels showing works of or by women, but she appears as a white shadow, empty but active, her studio clothes giving her a deceptively masculine silhouette. By making absence visible in this way Garrard helps to uncover the absence of history, of opportunity and of status that has dogged women artists, and now she continues to destabilise our faith in given certainties by exposing us to the friction of differing viewpoints and the collision of past and present.

Not only does she expose hidden agendas and attitudes, but Garrard's chosen method of documenting her work brings together unexpected realities and creates fault lines where surprising truths can burst through. Thus the Victoria & Albert's peculiar and very precise definitions of propriety in art were able to emerge as an unexpected by-product

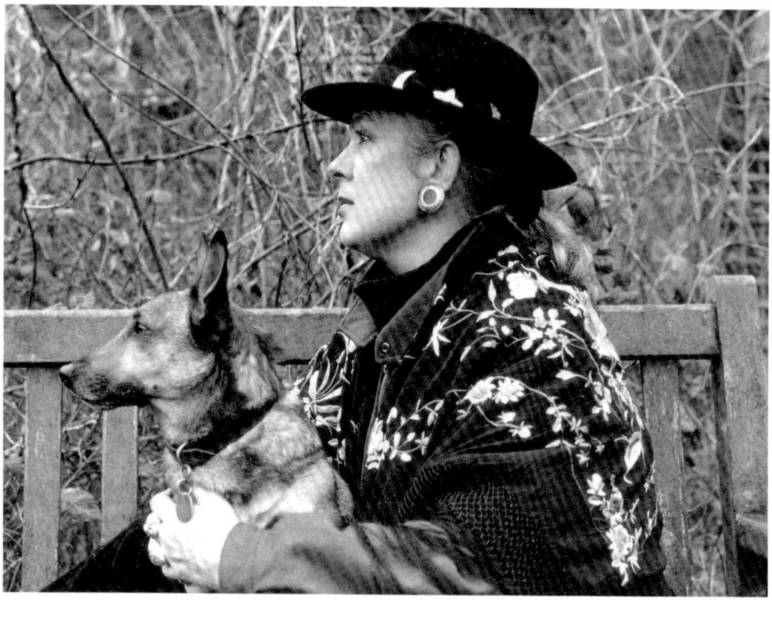

in the account of the museum's censorship of Garrard's 1974 'Universal Man in Forty Five Tasks' and were also summed up four years earlier when a young female by-stander interviewed by the Daily Mail in front of the half-covered female figures of 'Circle' in July 1970, declared "I mean, no one would take a second look at them if they were ordinary, unclothed dummies, would they?"

The relationship between Garrard's reading of gnostic texts and the visual richness of the works that she produced at this time, is one of many areas which are clarified and given new layers of meaning in this account of her art making. The figures which emerged from the pools of wash in 'Talisman' 1988 were not only part of her physical and psychological rehabilitation after a near-fatal motorbike accident, but they also represent Garrard consciously re-skilling herself at a key moment when her life and art, always in close association, became inseparable. But even while making the reader party to this very intimate information, Garrard never allows her voice to dominate, and consistently maintains that we are all equals trying to make sense of it all.

Creating room for the spectator to participate is not a new strategy for Garrard. Even before she started to make time-based work, audience input was crucial. She regarded her earliest projects such as 'Boundaries', where visitors walked amongst life sized figures on a ground of sand in a room of mirrors, or 'Horizon', where the reflections of spectators were an integral part of the work, as incomplete without the presence of outside observers; and more recently this relationship has become a primary factor in Garrard's practice. Her two residencies in Canada in 1991 and 1992, and now 'Exchanges for Empowerment' in Manchester in 1994, have all been dependent on a direct interaction between artist and public for their evolution, with Garrard reinstating the process of dialogue at the centre of the work, rather than trying to reach any kind of categorical agreement.

Garrard's refusal to be confined to a linear narrative or to a single critical interpretation of her practice is the inevitable response of an artist whose output has been devoted to the deconstruction of dogmatism. "All the way through, my work has been concerned with questioning the hard lines people draw around things. So when the soft model is wrapped by soft plaster, and then the plaster becomes hard, it becomes a shell, a protection, a container and a restriction." (Between Ourselves catalogue, 1984). Literally, metaphorically, and symbolically, Garrard represents women breaking out of their frames, satirising artistic genres and reclaiming their identities and pursuits. In 'Talisman', for example, she adapts the gnostic hymn The Thunder, Perfect Mind which celebrates the fragmentary co-existence of opposites and the duality inherent in the feminine principle; and it's no coincidence that Garrard has an enduring fascination with the Celtic interweave, yet another symbol of an alternative system that is fluid rather than static, and infinitely capable of re-inventing itself.

Garrard is unwilling to show work in a state fixed only by the past, as is usual in the traditional format of retrospective exhibitions. Apart from the fact that her work was not originally devised to take this form, and that many of her pieces were made in response to a particular context, a specific site and a set of circumstances; Garrard is also too questioning of the methods and motives of history to enter uncritically into this arena. Part of 'Casting Room One' 1986 involved her casting successive page 3 pin-ups from The Sun in plaster and at the same time modelling self-portrait heads of women artists, and setting the empty moulds into the newspaper panels. She then spent six days working in public and casting up positive heads of self portraits by women artists from the distorted clay pulled from the original moulds. By displaying this process and presenting the distorted positive casts alongside their original moulds Garrard re-asserted that history always sets down a biased view: "I'm owning up to the fact that in the act of replicating I cannot avoid distorting yet again".

Now, in order to dismantle this process, just as she has taken pains to include many voices and make the archiving of her own history as multifaceted as possible, so Garrard's current exhibition takes elements from past pieces and represents them in new configurations which emphasise other meanings and underline the potential mutability of her images and ideas. She has described her work as building blocks which can – and should – be deconstructed, re-arranged and re-assembled, and in this guise Garrard's art is well equipped to flow around the unyielding boundaries that can confront any artist whose work is absorbed into the mainstream, or the "manstream" as Garrard prefers to call it.

Of course, Garrard acknowledges that even the most factual of maps remains a highly subjective affair. Curves refuse to lie flat and remain accurate, and a vantage point has to be chosen from which the information is to be selected. But by refusing to fix her life and work to a series of absolutes, and by pointing out the multiple meanings of everything that we can – and cannot – see, Rose Garrard shows us that by retracing the meaning of our past steps, we can cover new ground in the future.

ARCHIVING MY OWN HISTORY

documentation of works 1969 > 1994

Photograph
Brian Blumer

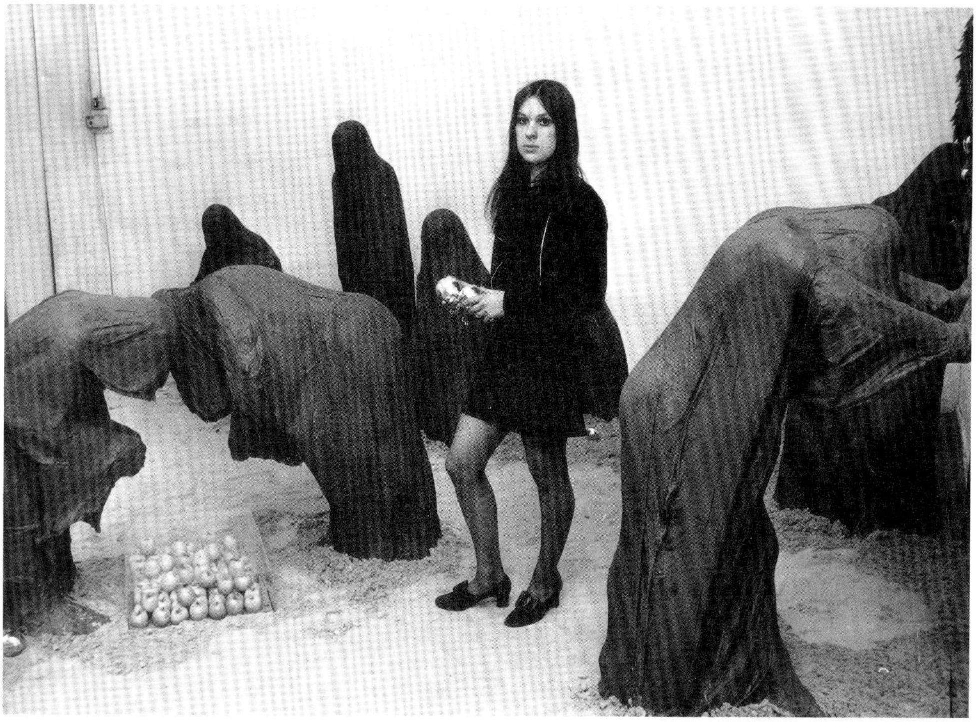

POPULAR PRESS But it is the sculpture here which will catch the eye, notably the whole room filled with blue-robed feminine figures, two of which bend disconsolately over a transparent box of apples, silver specimens of which also lie about the sanded floor. The exhibit has no title and even a talk with the artist did little to clarify what she has in mind except to credit viewers with more perception than most of us have. The only thing that really matters is that the work is strikingly imaginative and the effect, I thought, quite beautiful. Somebody should put it on view before it has to be broken up.
L.B.D. Birmingham Post, Saturday June 28 1969

ARTIST'S NOTES When I first went to Birmingham College of Art I wouldn't discuss my work as I was afraid to trust its subjective content to virtual strangers. One day the staff and students refused to allow me to leave the seminar room, barring the door until I would say what it was 'about'. I asked them to describe what aspect of the work this applied to and when they listed formal questions I exclaimed with relief 'Oh, is that all!'

Perhaps it would have been easier to discuss the more personal motivations behind the work with a female member of staff, but as was normal then, I had no tutoring from a woman artist at any time, on any course, and only the vaguest conscious awareness of this absence. Certainly the importance of the presence of appropriate female role models in educating women students was never realised, their absence from virtually all Art Colleges as lecturers or artists and their absence from the History of Art just weren't issues which we as students were aware of. But what this unspoken absence signified to us (and others) in terms of our own invisibility as potential artists, had begun to be absorbed by me and was reflected in the anonymous, covered female figures in 'Boundaries'. Consciously, this work attempted to alter the usual boundaries between the presence of the live spectator and the figurative 'sculptures' by various means, so that the visitor perceived that they were on and in the work, not separate from it. I was already concerned with the relationship of the spectator to art and was trying to identify and challenge outmoded concepts which limited art to fixed categories and spectators to a fixed role and distance from it, keeping each estranged from the other and denying the possibility of really being touched by art.
Rose Garrard 1994

SITE

'Graduate Show' Birmingham College of Art

COMPONENTS

24 life size plaster figures, scattered chrome apples, real apples in a perspex container, various wooden, metal and perspex structures related to figures all on a sand covered floor.

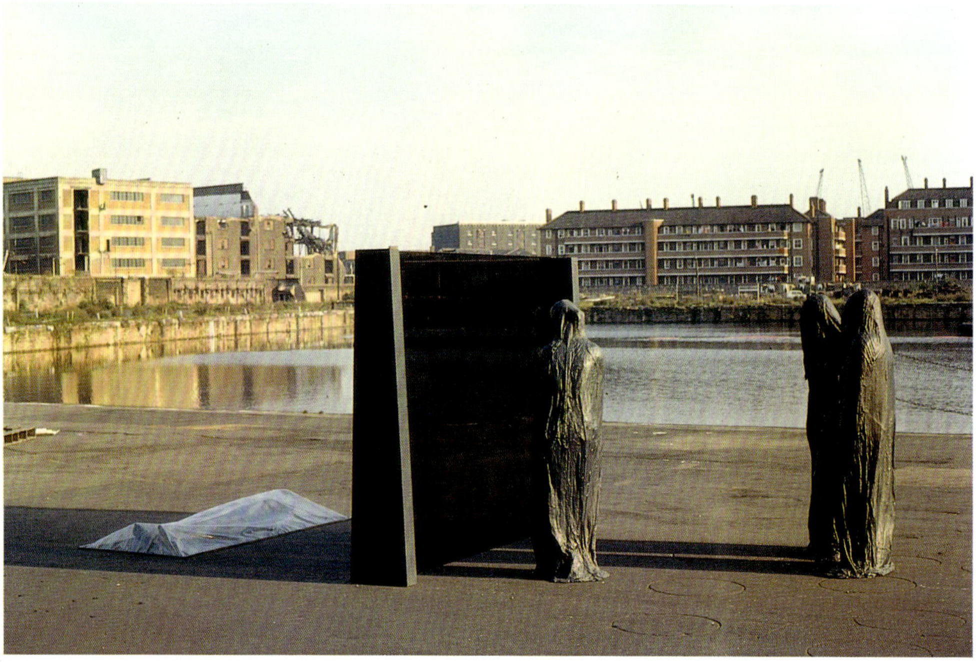

ART PRESS The sculpture is especially fascinating and none more so than Rose Garrard's 'Horizon' – a marvellous object consisting of an upright sheet of black, translucent perspex, on one side of which lies a cast of a nude woman, and on the other stand three shrouded female figures. The glass fuses the elements (including the observer) by transmitting or reflecting objects on either side of itself and is superbly disturbing.

Arts Review, May 1970

ARTIST'S NOTES On my first day of the Post-Graduate course I found I was one of eight sculpture students, with only one other woman. We talked and discovered we had each just got married, but were both apprehensive about disclosing this to the all male staff. To support each other we went together to tell the head of the course George Fullard, who was furious, but relatively speechless as he didn't seem able to put the reason for his anger into words.

Having a husband did reduce my social life in the evenings at college, which when combined with the intensity of my usual work pattern, was regarded as unfeminine behaviour by some. One staff member commented "So you're going to be a dyke like Frink ?" which I took to mean she had been a very committed worker while at Chelsea, though the inference that this was not considered a heterosexual way for a woman to work was not lost on me. I struggled to shake off the feeling of disempowerment, but it was a way of seeing the successful woman-as-artist which I never forgot.

The Kings Road was still part of the swinging sixties and walking down it each evening, my clothes covered in dust or encrusted with plaster and resin, I felt an outsider, not feminine enough for this fashion world, not masculine enough for the world of sculpture. The shop window reflections and this feeling of being watched and evaluated influenced the piece, though at the time I was most conscious and concerned to talk about the less personal level of content which dealt with the world-wide abuse of human rights.

'Horizon' was my first major piece here and I considered it whole only when spectators were present, seeing themselves occupying a voyeuristic role, witnessing the transfer of their own reflected image into the sculpture. Though divided in space the images unified in the screen and appeared to surround the fibreglass nude model who was lying veiled under a translucent cover. The search for 'an authentic female self beyond the empire of male signs' has engaged me ever since.

Rose Garrard 1994

SITES

'Post Graduate Show' Chelsea School of Art London

'First Show' Serpentine Gallery London

'Summer Summary' Alwin Gallery London

'Space Open Studios' St Katherine's Dock London

COMPONENTS

One lying fibreglass and three standing plaster figures with smoked perspex screen.

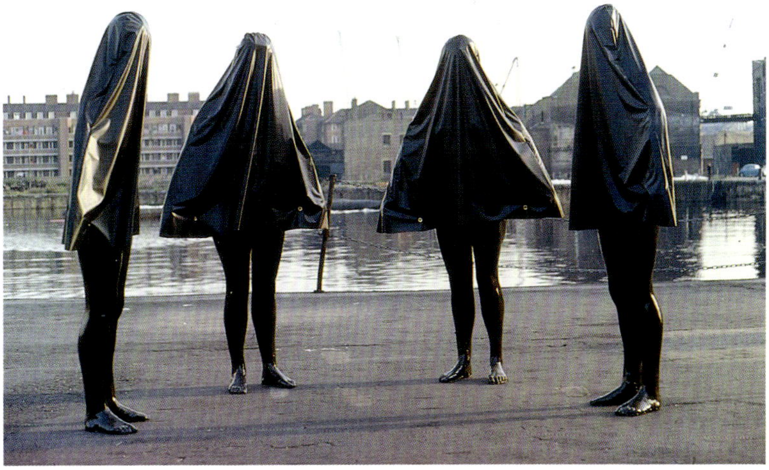

POPULAR PRESS Someone said it was art. And in a way they were right. It was a perfect exercise in the art of human reaction. The four 'nudes' appeared quite suddenly in Paternoster Square, in the shadow of St Paul's Cathedral. Dummies, of course. But shrouded in cloaks. Well, into yesterday's hot sunshine at lunchtime came the office crowds ... to gape ... to giggle ... to satisfy their curiosity. Some dared to sneak a peek under the cloaks, but many were too embarrassed. Others preferred to leave the illusion intact. But no-one passed without a second glance.

'Temp' Megs Carr, 26, from Blackheath, London, said: 'The idea is to make people want to know what's underneath, I suppose. I mean, no-one would take a second look at them if they were ordinary, unclothed dummies, would they?'

Daily Mail, Wednesday July 8 1970

ART PRESS The most successful and enigmatic of these early works is the outdoor 'Circle' 1970; four female figures, draped in covers which reach over their heads and down to their thighs, stand in a semi-circle. The anonymity here is not only imposing but terrifying; that Garrard should appropriate the devices of the horror story – concealment, exclusion, prohibition – is a clue to the darkening sense of absence and powerlessness the work seeks to convey. Just as reading against the grain in children's fiction produces a series of dispiriting sexual stereotypes of patriarchal violence, these figures belie their own fictional 'innocence'. Their very self-effacement gives them the appearance of Victim, of Other, of figures from the realm of the untouchable. In these works Garrard is speaking through the body by denying its physical existence; these hooded, featureless women are bodiless because they have no real female models to call upon.

John Roberts, 'Between Ourselves', Ikon Gallery, Birmingham, 1984

ARTIST'S NOTES 'Circle', conceived as a repeat unit multiple of four or more figures, always included one gap to indicate to the spectator that they could enter inside or link up the circle. This combination of live and static human presences was in part a desire for unity in response to the increasing levels of state violence which met student protests in Europe and America at that time. The piece caused much comment when in a strange coincidence four students were shot and killed at Kent State University while it was being shown at the Serpentine Gallery, and it was removed from the Dublin Gallery window where people saw it as a direct reference to the 'troubles'. The mini skirted shrouds were a deliberate subversion of the then current obsession with womens legs, exemplified in Claes Oldenburg's cooling tower/womens knees multiples. Before my interview for the course at Chelsea I was advised that if I wanted a real chance I should wear a mini-skirt not trousers and shouldn't admit to having a regular boyfriend. I complied and gained a place, but the mood of this piece registers the personal cost of these negative experiences by powerfully visualising my own sense of being seen as 'a sex object' rather than as a sculptor. The Daily Mail newspaper published a photo of 'Circle' with a mini-skirted passer by bending over in front of the camera to lift up their coverings. I replied by repeat copying the mini skirted woman, collaging them to form a circle lifting their own skirts, and suggesting that they print this instead. The paper sent a letter of apology for taking the piece so lightly, and surprisingly, of encouragement to do more work.

Rose Garrard 1994

SITES

'First Show' Serpentine Gallery London

'Summer Summary' Alwin Gallery London

'Triangle' TUC Headquarters Congress House London

'London Now' Messenhallen West Berlin

'Spring in the Air' Hugh Lane Municipal Art Gallery Dublin

COMPONENTS

Multiple of life size figure repeat unit in resin and fibreglass with PVC covers

COLLECTION

First four units sold by the Alwin Gallery London to anonymous Swiss collector.

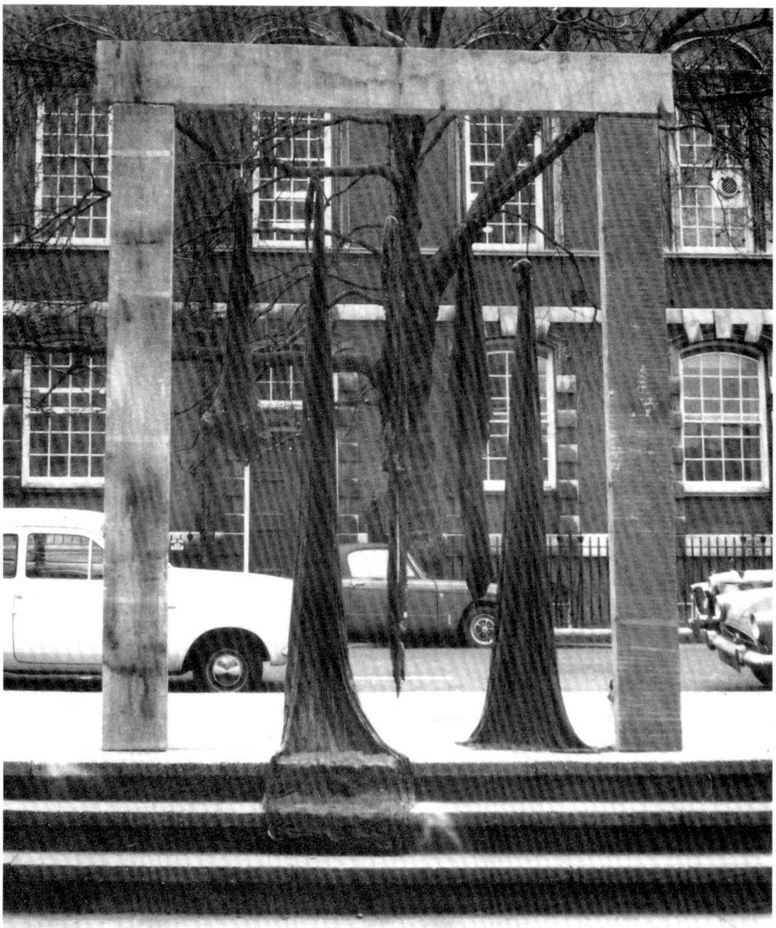

ARTIST'S NOTES After working at Birmingham College of Art with no funds for materials or equipment and few visiting staff, but with a large, individual studio space, the relative economic wealth of Chelsea School of Art came as a shock. It seemed ironic that the situation was now reversed, with a tiny work space shared by eight students but plenty of materials, equipment, machining workshops and technical support. It felt unrealistic to totally abandon the practical, economic ways of working I had developed out of necessity, in favour of more technically dependent practices that I would probably have difficulty sustaining after leaving college. I concentrated on improving my casting and construction skills, learnt etching and created some deliberately transient works outside the confined studio space.

'Threshold' was one of four 'street interventions' which I installed anonymously, without permission, on pavements in and near the Kings Road during 1970. Each was put in place for only one day, quickly sited in the early morning, abandoned for the day and dismantled again at night. This felt very empowering, like a guerilla activity, leaving unexpected art objects to be encountered as new incidents in the street's routine daily life.

Rose Garrard 1994

SITE

Kings Road Chelsea London

COMPONENTS

Wooden structure with hessian and plaster hangings.

Photograph
A Fleury

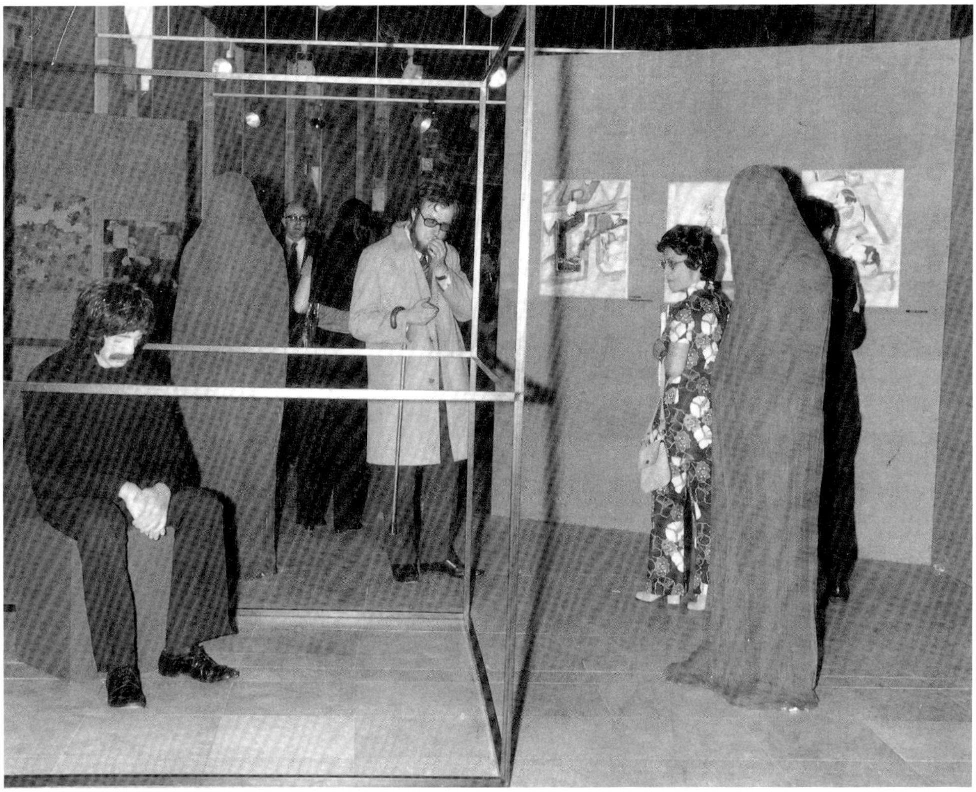

ARTIST'S NOTES When I arrived in Paris on a one year scholarship I was refused the allocated studio and accommodation at the Cité des Arts because my husband, artist Kerry Trengove was to live with me. At first we had to stay in a very cheap hotel and as our money ran out we would walk round and round the outside of the Grand Magazins at closing time, picking up centimes dropped in the rubbish from the street stalls. This was usually enough to buy bread, cheese, a tomato and bottle of wine, which was our diet until my grant arrived six weeks later.

I asked some French friends if I could work in their garage space as I had no studio, so they kindly parked their car in the street for the rest of the year. At first I made a number of drawings, collages, and temporary street figures in plaster, but discovered that I couldn't be reimbursed for these as the scholarship fund only covered 'special' materials. In this piece, 'Cube', I wanted to change the gender of the central subject being watched to male, and to contain the figure in a defined volume to suggest territory he occupied yet was confined to. As I began planning this work I realised I couldn't afford to make it unless, ironically, I used more expensive materials to ensure that I would be reimbursed.

I'd already become very interested in waxworks, a popular sculptural tradition in Paris, and persuaded the sculptor at the Musée Grevin to tell me some trade secrets, including the name of their wax supplier. They then told me the proportions necessary to make a portrait head and as I had so little money the model this time had to be my husband Kerry Trengove. The fund would pay for the wax and the dexion cube, and the three standing sentinels were made from the remaining plaster. These surrounded the seated wax figure, and on the fourth side, outlines of feet indicated the ideal viewing position for a participating spectator. I arrived late for the exhibition opening to find a drunken man inside the cube trying to prize open the figure's fragile wax hands and insert a wine glass. Using my worst street French I asked him to stop, but as he emerged he told me he was a Judge for the Prix D'Honneur de Paris and had been waiting for me as I had won the Gold Medal for sculpture. Though I was given the certificate I never actually received the medal and left for England soon after this. I was however offered studios, grants and exhibitions by the same bureaucrats whose earlier decisions had reduced us to hunger and poverty, but by now I'd had enough of such double standards and couldn't wait to be back in London.

Rose Garrard 1994

SITE

'International Exhibition of Artistes Etrangers' ORTF Centre Paris

COMPONENTS

One wax and three plaster figures, dexion cube. Made during French Government Scholarship through the British Council, to study sculpture as an élèwve libre at the Ecole des Beaux Arts Paris

AWARD

Prix D'Honneur de Paris for Sculpture.

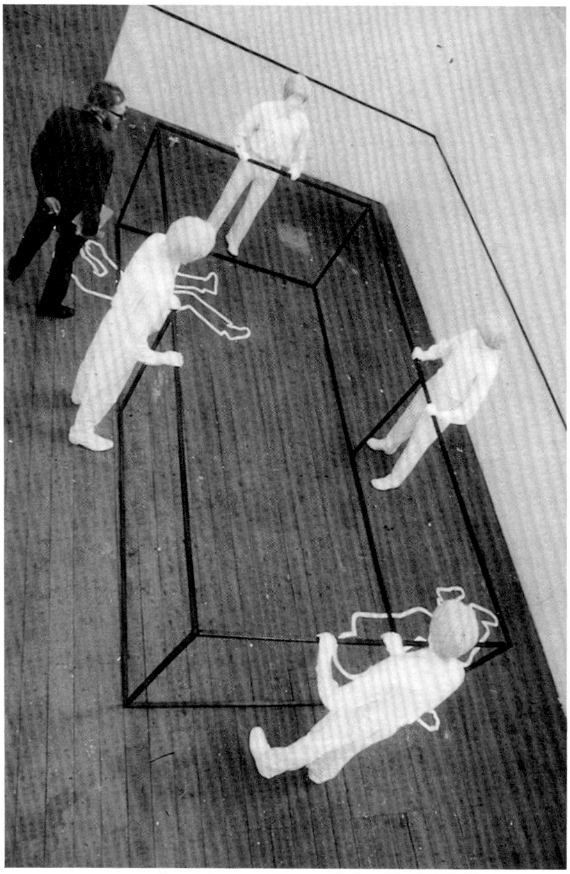

ARTIST'S NOTES We returned from Paris completely penniless to find Britain was deep in recession and that, for the first time, there were over one million unemployed. Having found a tiny flat in Brixton, I began work on 'Parallel' in the confines of the lounge. Though I had been invited to make a piece for the 'Spectrum' exhibition there were no funds for materials and I so worked discontentedly in chicken wire and papier maché to make the four life size male figures. Meanwhile the Alwin Gallery claimed an irreversible clerical error when I protested that their cheque for the sale of 'Circle' to a Swiss collector, was for less than half of the small sum they had originally agreed to pay me for the piece. This meant I had hardly covered the cost of materials and this episode reinforced my fears and reservations about dealings with the commercial gallery system. This and other events, such as not being able to afford to travel to private views of my own work outside London, led me to begin a deep reassessment of my habitual relationship to the making, showing and selling of art objects. I began to look for a way to 'liberate' my work from the constraints put on it by commercial demands, and decided to develop another source of income to fund it.
Rose Garrard 1994

Quietly separated from my Fine Art work were the freelance commercial activities which helped finance it. Commissions for theatre, television, magazines and architects. Work which involved image and object making, and dramatic changes in scale. Unlike my Fine Art work these objects were not valued by their owners for their investment potential, but solely for their ability to express an idea. To create them often involved an apparently disproportionate amount of time, effort and skill relative to their usually limited existence. They were also often put into contexts that extended their original meaning through the addition of elements such as sound, lighting and installation. Slowly I began to feel that the self-made 'rules' which had evolved around my work as a sculptor were confining me to a predictable future form and direction.
Rose Garrard, 'Lives', Arts Council of Great Britain, 1979

SITE

'Art Spectrum' Alexandra Palace London

COMPONENTS

Four standing figures surrounding dexion enclosure with white outlined figures painted on floor.

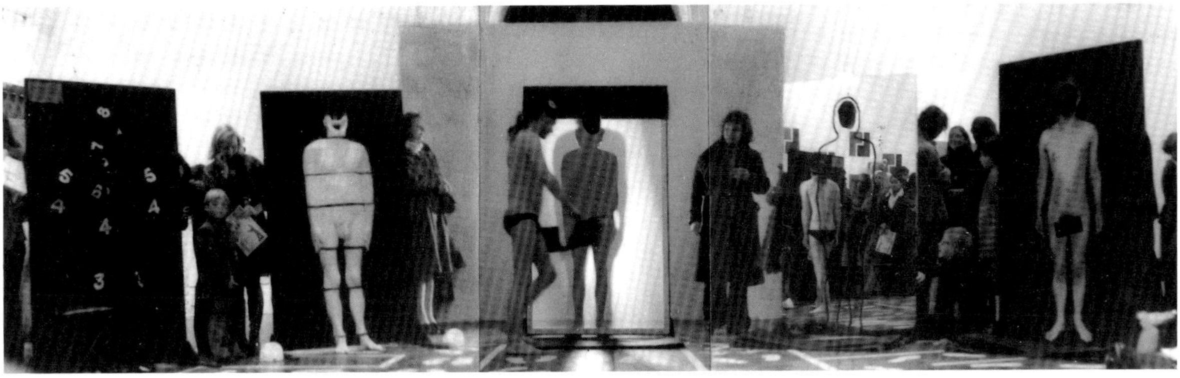

ARTIST'S NOTES The idea of the 'Body Box' show was to explore the ways in which the human body had been represented in art and life. It was planned to contain a variety of objects and images including paintings, photographs, life casts, clothing and sculpture. I saw the commission as an opportunity to make a time-based work linking some of these diverse media in one piece, and relating the work to some particular exhibits.

I named my new work 'Universal Man' in response to the inclusion in the exhibition of the muscle-bound, macho figure of Mr Universe. This life cast, a complete-in-every-detail nude, personified the idealised sexual stereotype of masculine strength. In contrast, my concern was to present 'ordinary man' and to have him physically construct and then deconstruct his less glamourous image, represented here by his shadow, his reflection, his suit of clothes, his body cast and his photograph.

These actions were conceived as a series of tasks which would be carried out continuously throughout the opening of the exhibition, as if it was a 'live sculpture'. The numbered sequence of actions, assembling and uncovering, then dissassembling and covering sections of objects, images and the performer himself, were to be carried out evenly and cyclically, without a sense of drama or personal gesture,and without emphasis on a beginning or end. Visitors could predict the continuation of the process and so walk away, 'seeing it in passing' rather than stopping to watch.

While installing the piece in the 'Body Box' exhibition it attracted a great deal of interest from the staff at the Victoria & Albert Museum. At first this seemed very welcome, but after a couple of days I was told that rumours had been circulating around the Museum that 'this woman artist is presenting a male strip-tease act!' As a consequence the Director Roy Strong had felt that it should be previewed by four staff who had already decided, on the basis of the gossip, that they were against it, and four staff who were for it.

That evening this already prejudiced group sat through one complete two hour cycle of the work, deciding to censor it in various ways and requesting that the piece be reduced to this one cycle only. They insisted that the genitals on the black and white photograph had to be covered, though those on the plaster life casts did not, and that the performer should not be naked. As much as I was concerned that such changes would destroy the integrity of the piece, I was also fascinated by the identification of these particular limits, by which the institution made visible its usually invisible boundaries of propriety in art, (the V & A houses a large collection of antique erotica). Responding to their flippant proposal that the required coverings should be diamante fig leaves, I suggested that perhaps a suitable compromise would be to hang a plaster cast set of genitals to mask the two dimensional image. This wasn't acceptable ... but the staff seemed disappointed that I did choose to use the statutary black censorship oblong and black briefs to fulfil their requirements.

Rose Garrard 1994

SITE

'Body Box' Victoria & Albert Museum London

COMPONENTS

Five six foot high screens, five life size representations of a human male; segmented numbered clothing and plaster casts, segmented numbered coverings over photograph, mirror and shadow. 45 tasks, assembling objects and uncovering images, performed by Genesis P. Orridge

COMMISSION

Victoria & Albert Museum London.

POWER PORTRAITS AND GIFTS

Photograph Andrew Putler

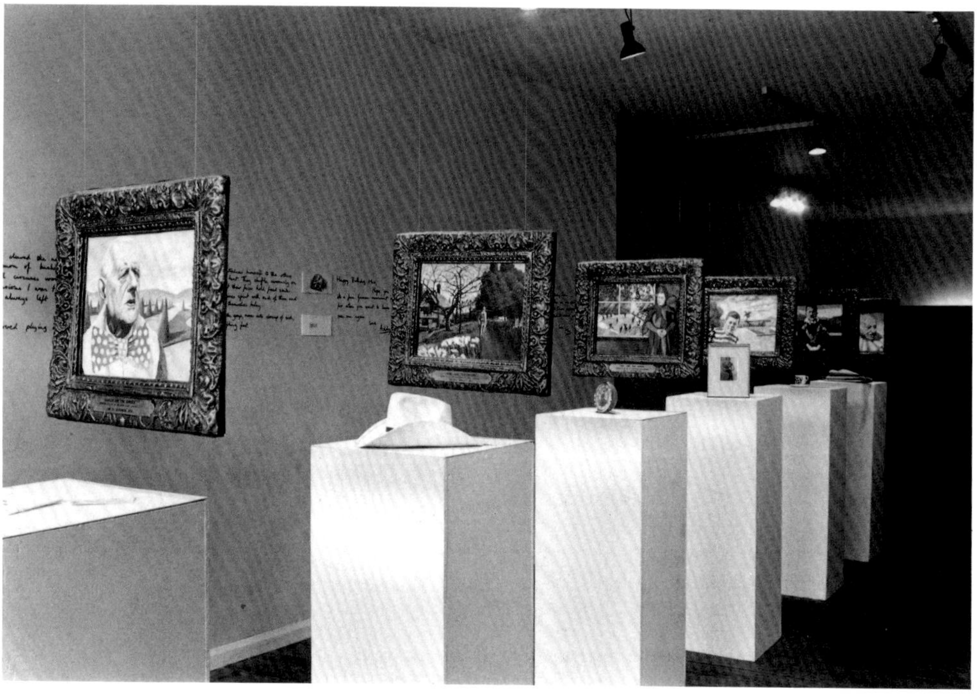

ARTIST'S NOTES Three years and fifteen exhibitions beyond my formal art training I stopped. I stopped trying to make 'sculpture', I stopped trying to make 'paintings'. I stopped showing. I stopped trying to compartmentalise my interests.

I began to look at what made life exciting for me. I began to research, interviewing, reading, drawing, writing, putting ideas down in whatever form seemed most appropriate, in whatever media expressed them best. Gradually the question of what art could be took precedence over what art was. In trying to locate this threshold the examination of stereotypes (both artistic and personal) emerged as a primary interest. The apparent meaning, function and worth of objects and images, the particular language of form and value attached to Fine Art objects, their role, my role as an artist and a woman in relation to them. Major concerns in my earlier sculptural work, form/perception, appearance/reality, representation/identity, took on new life.

Rose Garrard, 'Lives', Arts Council of Great Britain, 1979

POPULAR PRESS Should you happen to step into the Acme Gallery, Covent Garden, one morning during the next three weeks – beware! A surprise awaits you. Wander past a column of portraits – featuring Hitler, Churchill, Gandhi, Kennedy, Mao and de Gaulle – towards a painted wall and a wooden gate. Look around the corner and there before you, you will see a petite curly haired woman gazing intently into a neon lit mirror. Stroke by stroke, she is banishing her fair skin and curls for the macabre guise of a circus clown; white face, white skull and glittering costume.

John Spearman, West London Observer, May 26 1977

POPULAR PRESS Apart from anything else they may have had in common, Hitler and Churchill both liked to think of themselves as artists. The art of oratory, the art of war, even the art of leadership it seems were not enough. They had to have a go at the real thing too: art as done by painters.

Nobody cares for Hitler's art anymore, and perhaps they never did. But Churchill won the war and his canvases (on show at M. Knoedler and Co Ltd, 143 New Bond Street) fetch high prices as we know; though perhaps his undoubted skill in the other arts he practiced has more to do with this than his painting. Not that he left them altogether behind when he went painting. He liked to set up in front of the motif, back to back with his batman who would squeeze the yellow ochre onto the palette when needed. Such peculiarities are the starting point for Rose Garrard's elaborate explorations of the masked natures of the great dictators or the men of power, depending on how you look at them. ...The effect is striking at first and certainly makes you remember how unobjectively history is written.

Caroline Tisdall, The Guardian, May 23 1977

RANDOM DIALOGUES ON THE MONUMENT

Photograph
Andrew Putler

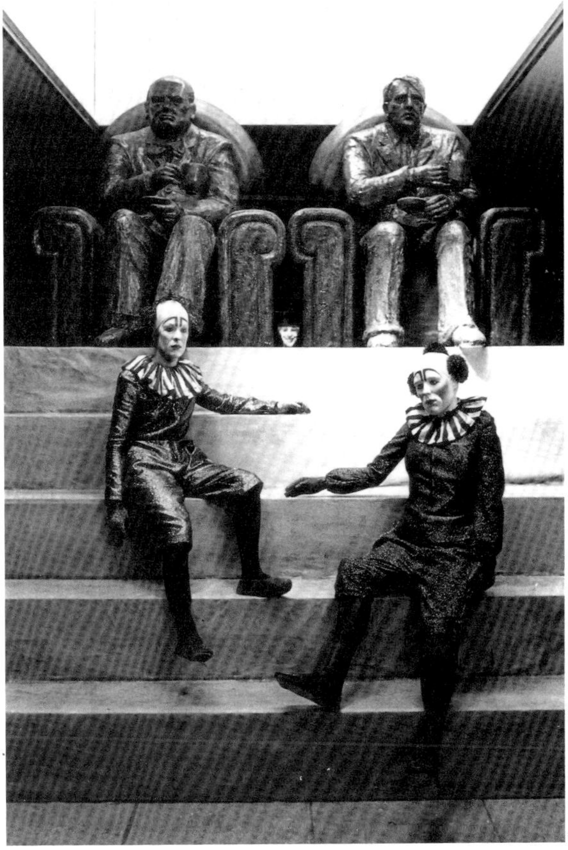

ART PRESS This was the break-through point at which she brought together all her interests and abilities to form a coherent and self-fulfilling whole. Garrard used the two floors of the gallery as connecting spaces, both literally and metaphorically. In the upper space the installation took the form of a garden (with artificial grass, brick walls, and canvas paving stones) at the end of which stood the severe but none the less risible statues of Hitler and Churchill seated in armchairs, drinking tea; behind this 'Monument' was a continuous playing video 'Smile Please', accompanied by military music, that showed Garrard, made-up as a clown, twisting her face into a smile. In the lower space she had constructed a circus dressing-room, partitioned off by a garden wall, that contained ventriloquist dummies of Churchill and Hitler; also a dolls-house inside the gallery window, visible from outside, the garden space of which was a miniature version of that in the upper gallery; and further, there were six portaits of world leaders (de Gaulle, Kennedy, Mao, Gandhi, Hitler, Churchill) painted, framed and hung between plinths that supported imagined gifts from one leader to another.

The installation/performance lasted for three weeks. Each day began with Garrard making up as a clown in the gallery. This was her ritual initiation, her symbolic entry into the contradictions of her created world. During the day she would methodically build 'The Wall' with bricks, and perform 'Random Dialogue', various improvisations with a mannequin of herself, as well as invigilating and talking to the pass-through audience. This sense of the artist being active as an object of identification within the work was most direct in a twice-weekly scripted performance 'Set Piece', which consisted of her manipulating the dummies of Hitler and Churchill to an audio-tape of personal details and biographical quotations on the two leaders from various authors. The histories of these two figures, their aspirations to be artists (one unsuccess-fully, the other on a Sunday-painter basis) supplies the symbolic confrontation in the work between desire and discipline. Monumentalised but domesticated, the will-to-power and the legitimisation of violence represented by these authority figures and artists manque becomes bathetic; by reducing their presence to tricks of stage-craft, Garrard subjects their 'love of art' and their politics to the same banal level. The use of mime, Garrard's clown persona, the statues and ornate garden, all indicate a dreamscape, and as in all dreams certain figures and objects are the products of displacement. The psychological content of the earlier work – the pressure of roles, the sense of suffocation – has been extended to treating the wider theme of paternal law; for the first time specific autobiographical material becomes the basis for an imaginative re-entry into the past. The work represents an explosion of signification, a massive clearing-house for all the disparate, half-articulated feelings Garrard had been working through previously; there was a clear sense of wanting to tell all, of wanting everything to fit together, to create analogous patterns of meaning between events and objects.

John Roberts,'Between Ourselves', Ikon Gallery, Birmingham, 1984

DIVIDING WALL

Photograph
Andrew Putler

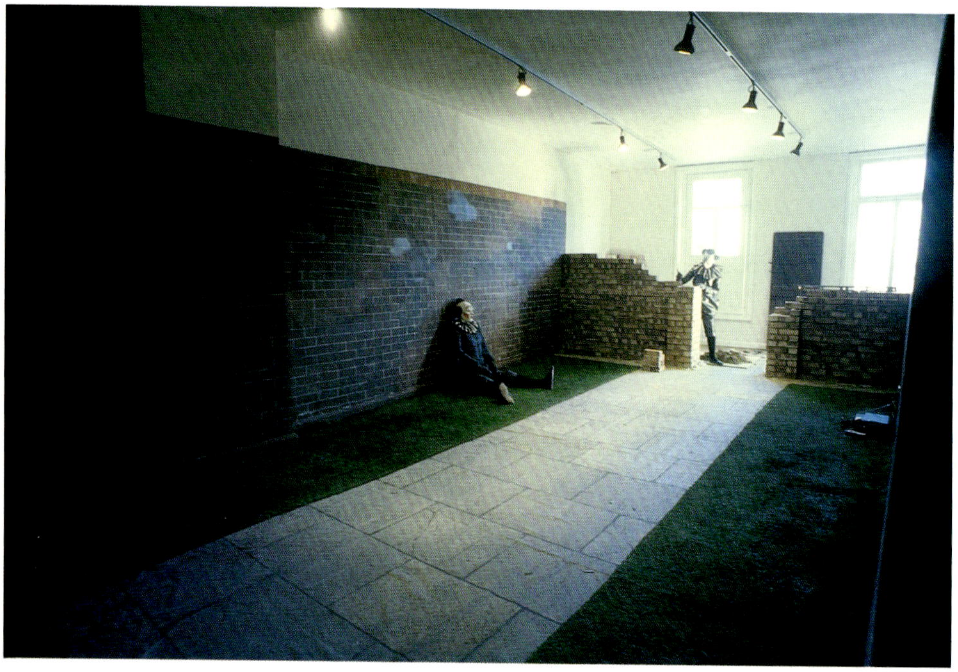

PRESS RELEASE What is remarkable over and above the combination of these things is the consistency in strength and decisiveness of the imagery, and the immaculateness and professionalism in construction of all the objects involved. They all have sufficient authority or plausibility to create a whole which is undeniably real but of Rose's making, and therefore entirely subject to her manipulation, as indeed are the archetypal power-figures which are manipulated dummies.

The above description is necessarily inadequate, partly because one does not wish to give the game away too soon. Each set of objects are capable of sustaining separate viewing on their own, and hold surprises and present paradoxes for and to the spectator as they transcend traditional ideas about 'painting' and 'sculpture', and take one through from apparent to actual realities.

Jonathan Harvey, Acme Gallery, London, May 1977

ART PRESS 'Incidents in a Garden' is a work in which the past and its confusions become subject to the exigencies of the present; and one in which Garrard's performing, her manipulation of the figures, her role-changing, becomes, in the face of the will-to-power of male representation a gesture of emancipation. Transformed into stage-props, these male authority-figures have been brought into a world constructed on Garrard's terms. Ludic celebration, garden of personal rememberance, exorcism of male roles, the work was a staging of vulnerability over power. As a spectacular finale to the work and as an extension of its openness, during the final week Garrard had invited eight artists from various disciplines to perform in the space. On the last night dancers from the Royal Ballet, having danced the politicians, systematically destroyed the downstairs installation.

This remarkably imaginative and energetic work initiated Garrard's examination of the personal through the use of narrative and myth; it represented the point in her work where the personal and the social coalesce; and it was where she began to elaborate on the idea of frames, on the 'mockery of frames'.

John Roberts, 'Between Ourselves', Ikon Gallery, Birmingham, 1984

SITE

'Incidents in a Garden' Acme Gallery London

COMPONENTS

Lower Gallery. six paintings of male archetypes in vacuum formed frames, 'Power House' dolls house with six miniature figures, 'Gifts' six domestic objects on plinths, 'Flat' low relief panel of section of wall and door, 'Set Piece' sawdust ring, dressing table and mirror, two ventriloquist soft sculpture figures, with scripted live action to audio-tape once each week.'Story Board' continuous strip around gallery walls comprising photos, text, drawings, coloured illustrations and hand written script for imaginary film. All objects have tie-on labels as film props.

Upper Gallery: 'Dividing Wall' actual brick wall and replica garden door, built across gallery throughout the three weeks as a task-based durational live work, 'Random Dialogues' improvised performances daily with articulated lifesize fibreglass clown figure,'Monument' in carved polystyrene with bronze patina of Hitler and Churchill seated in armchairs having tea, with visible fixing instructions, painted canvas paved pathway, artificial grass, walls painted as brickwork, and 'Smile Please' continuous play black and white video. Invited Individual Evening Performances by:

1 Peter Butcher (Behavioural Psychologist)

2 Brian Routh (of Kipper Kids performance duo)

3 Marilyn Halford and William Raban (Filmmakers)

4 Tina Keane (Multi-media artist)

5 David Drew (Choreographer) and Royal Ballet School students

6 Ron Haselden and Stephen Ricketts (Multi-media artists).

Photograph
Ian Potter

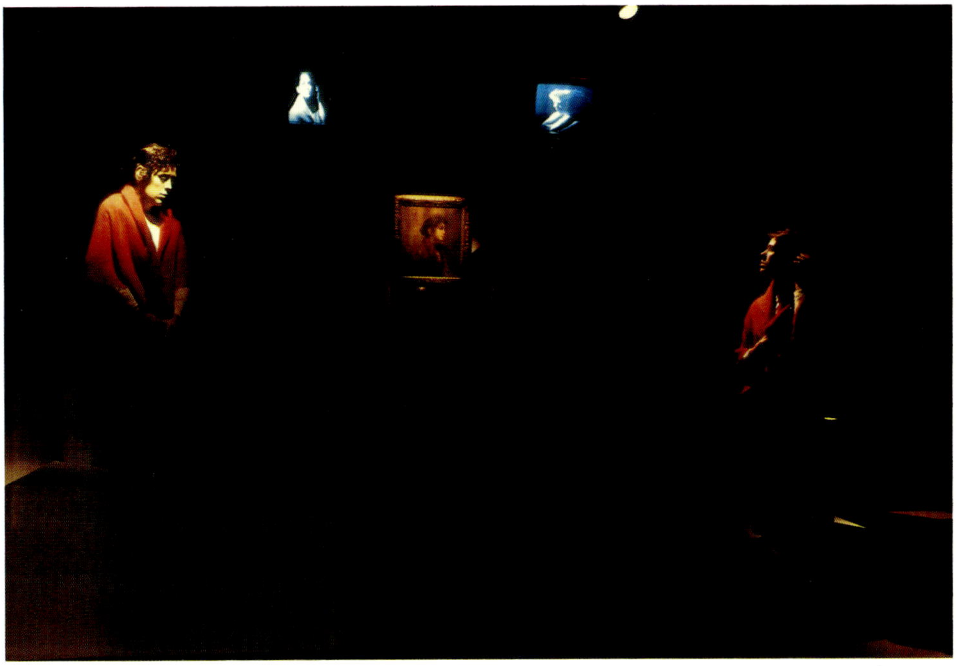

ART PRESS 'Surveillance' operates on a principal of exponential growth in meaning which happens on many levels simultaneously, both in what is being revealed, and in the medium of its expression. The title is an example of this rendering a wealth of significance and word-play. So is the way in which Garrard plays with space, moving from two dimensions to three, to the multiples created by video, and then stretching this framework of space into her own past and future with the subject matter of the work, her personal history and her exploration of self-images. The same observations can be made of her presentation of time, for the biographical material is elusive because it's fast moving and full of double meanings, and the sound tape and video facilitate a complex use of synchronised time-delay, structurally (what we hear is different from what we see) and referentially (past, present and future)
But the revelation of self-imagery is only the starting point of 'Surveillance'. It has the characteristic strength of much women's art to illuminate public issues through the focus of private experience. And, again, the structure facilitates this in a direct and economical way. Images of women necessarily predominate, but the examination of female identity comprehends the male role (as father, portrait painter, art historian who assumes the picture to be painted by a man, as 'other', as male painter of women). Images of women on video key instantly into cultural role-play, advertising and the media. The personal language of dress, of dressing up for social roles, of projecting a desired identity or feeling trapped within one are also inseparable from the industries and media which use (or abuse) this language ...
If 'Surveillance' can be said to be about anything, it is about power and the manipulation of power through signs and communication systems, and like the most successful radical practitioners in other fields, Garrard achieves purity (the freedom of the expert to pursue knowledge as far as is possible) and social accessibility (in the radical sense) simultaneously without uneasy division. Her conversation after the performance centred round two issues, her gender and her willingness to confront ambiguity, and she was clear that she works in an area which is beyond gender, beyond the exclusive categories of sexual politics in the same way that she has moved away from the traditional restrictive practices of painting and sculpture. That her long standing interest in the arts of self image making, and image projection is used to raise questions not to answer them; to facilitate understanding, not to make judgements. And that her interest in ambiguity is in its power to reveal truths not to mask them. This did communicate during the performance by her presentation of self, not only a manipulator of power, but as a person upon whom power has a manipulative effect. Victim as well as hero, caught in the network of lines as well as creator of it. Exploder of mysteries of social control.
Dinah Dossor, Performance, January 1981

ARTIST'S NOTES The space is in heavy shadow. A painting of a young woman hangs in a shaft of sunlight in the hall, opposite the window. The painting used to hang in the hall, or was it the kitchen? It was not the best painting in the house. It is unsigned, unfinished, and damaged. But it is the painting I chose to take with me when I left.
The 'key' object in this installation is the 19th century framed portrait, which becomes both the subject matter and the content of the work. The word 'Concours' – competitive examination – which is written on the canvas, triggered memories of competitiveness and lack of it, perfection and imperfection, and role playing in my own upbringing. These were supplemented by my feelings as an artist (active surveyor) and as a young girl (passive model), which were clarified by trying to objectify why I had chosen to take that particular painting with me when I left home. I named the piece 'Surveillance'.
Rose Garrard, 'Lives', Arts Council of Great Britain, 1979

Photograph
Pierret

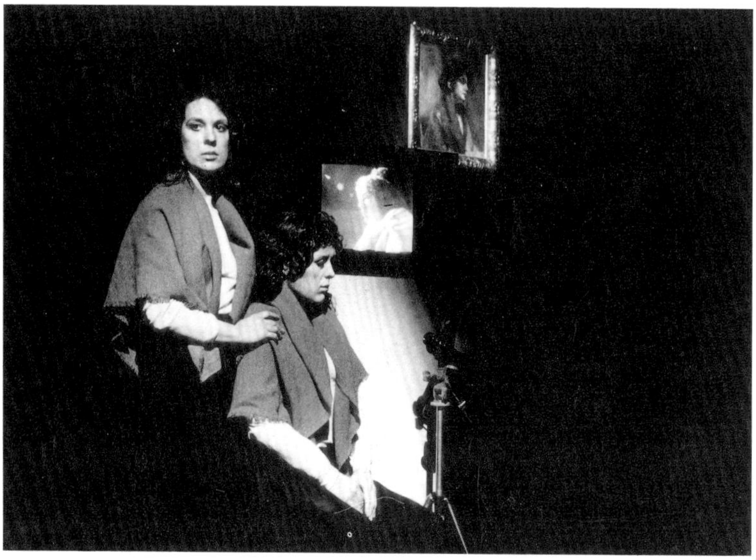

ART PRESS 'Surveillance' is premised on a single autobiographical incident, image, object; an anonymous portrait of a woman presented to her by her mother when Garrard left home to become an artist ... As a gift the painting came to represent for Garrard an exchange of values, an investment in her of what she saw in the work – male aspirations to greatness and female aspirations to be visible. It becomes the representational model – the frame through which Garrard presents her capture by, and escape from, certain expectations ... For Garrard, the anonymous portrait-as-present had become the 'script' for addressing and clarifying her status and function as a woman and as an artist.

As before Garrard uses various media ... but in this instance they were subject to a specific organising principle; the portrait and its ideological framework as a questionable role-model ... The work becomes a model of representational closure; Garrard displays herself as that which is framed, that which is represented, as well as that which represents. Garrard's script presents a self-reflexive account of herself as the object of the gaze of others (of audience) "Control the pace of your movements. Walk like the model, keep your head up. Try not to look tense. Try not to stumble when you climb to your seat. If necessary pretend the spectators aren't there." Her live, spoken script, an intentionally hesitant monologue, is offset by an authorial male counterpart giving a National Gallery historio-critical evaluation of the portrait. The male voice complements the action of the television camera, probing and hypothesising, increasing the sense of unease and manipulation. That he immediately assumes the portrait artist to have been male, unwittingly contributes to the sense of predetermination that the work plays on; whatever the sex of the painter it is secondary to the symbolic power of the absent author. If we see the painting as made by a man then it confirms its curatorial and commercial status within the signifying framework; if we see the painting as that made by a woman (the absence of signature and the 'unfinished' quality could give credence to this) then it becomes an object reclaimed, a cause for celebration. Whichever, the consequence is positive.

John Roberts, 'Between Ourselves', Ikon Gallery, Birmingham, 1984

ARTIST'S NOTES In recognising how closely I identified with the subject I realised that the spectators could be fused into the work by illuminating their role as passive surveyors and active evaluators. My intention was to risk revealing intimate personal details of my life which relate directly to the portrait, and in completing a task which I had never previously attempted (speaking publicly from a precise learned script), risked doing this 'imperfectly'. These activities paralleled the vulnerable role of the model. As artist and instigator of the situation, I took command by predicting on tape my own appearance, the audiences reaction and so on. This I felt would create an atmosphere of tension in which the audience would be oscillating between concern for me as a person and criticism of me as an artist/performer.

Preceding these subjective memories a male voice (an art historian from the National Gallery), is heard giving a rational, objective breakdown of the painting in art historical terms. The question of its apparent worth in aesthetic, artistic and monetary terms were discussed, issues of interest to me as these traditionally effect the evaluation of art work. The revelation of 'new meanings', another value system based on personal experience (my memories), opens up new interpretations for the spectator and focuses attention back to the portrait as a metaphor for male and female role-playing.

Rose Garrard, 'Lives', Arts Council of Great Britain, 1979

SITES

'Hayward Annual' Hayward Gallery London

'Lives' Arts Council Purchase exhibition Serpentine Gallery London

Chapter Arts Centre Cardiff Wales

'Symposium of International Performance' Lyon France

COMPONENTS

Script, soundtrack, painted portrait and life-size fibreglass and resin figure/model, two surveillance cameras linked to two monitors. Artist as model and performer

COLLECTION

Arts Council of Great Britain 1979.

Photograph of Performer/spectator Kevin Atherton

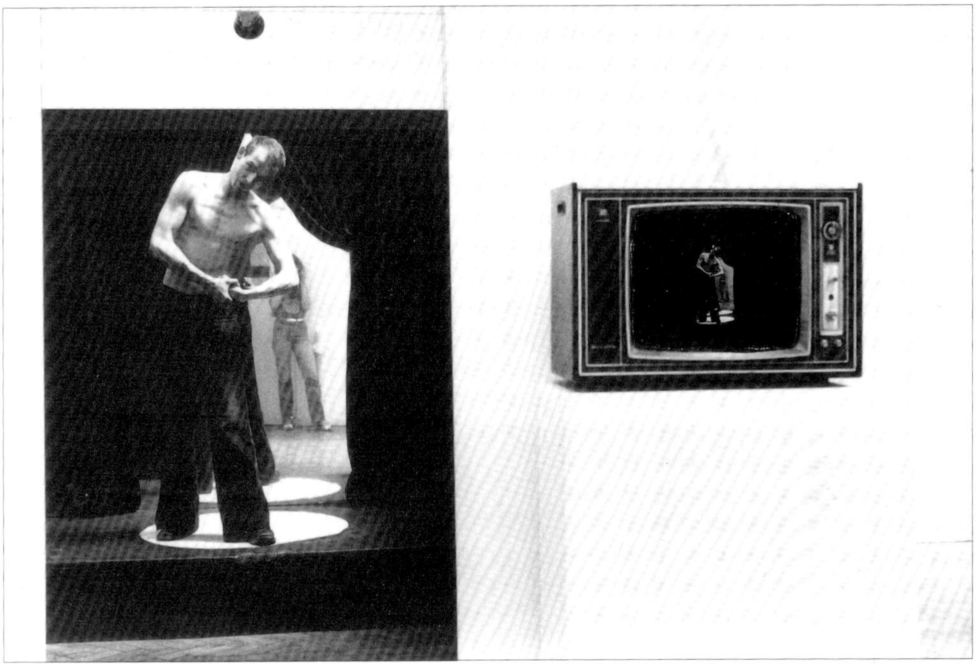

ARTIST'S NOTES 'Towards a New Heroism' created for the Whitechapel Art Gallery 'Art for Society' exhibition, was a simple black room and a small spotlit stage with black silk curtains facing the entrance. The curtains were drawn slightly back to reveal a mirror reflecting the viewer's image. The mirror image was surveyed continuously by a close-circuit video camera, and the picture relayed to a monitor which could only be seen from outside the entrance.

Many visitors, knowing that their actions, if performed before the mirror, would be monitored to anyone outside the installation, often could not resist the attraction of the 'spotlight'. Their activities took place in the context of a continuous-play audio tape of extracts from documentary, cinema and TV film soundtracks, in which classic gender stereotyped characters and situations occurred. These extracts were structured into an ironic narrative, with my own voice 'directing', giving instructions towards the 'perfect' performance. In this way the continual propagation of stereotyped gender role-playing by the media was brought to the listeners attention. The mild humour with which visitors were encouraged to participate in this 'game' was countered by two short quotations (on opposite side walls) from the husband/wife respectively of a famous show-business partner.

"Suddenly a gong went off in my head. I realised that whatever I wanted in life I'd better start trying to grab ...
I don't want to read about someone elses experiences. I want my own. I want to be more myself and less Mrs ...... I'm independent and sure of myself now."
Paul Newman's wife Joanne.

"She was a success and suggested that if I wanted I could give up my job. At first I rejected the idea ... It seemed difficult – being the husband of the woman who is the prime bread-winner, and now I'm actually doing what I've always wanted to do. And yes, its marvellous."
Claire Rayner's husband Desmond.

These texts were concerned with the real problems of individual fulfilment beyond the traditional limits of gender roles. Two identical miniature models of the installation displayed just inside the entrance, posed two short questions on the restrictions of conditioned masculine and feminine behaviour.

Rose Garrard 1994

SITE

'Art for Society' Whitechapel Art Gallery London

COMPONENTS

15ft x 12ft enclosed space, surveillance camera linked to external monitor, 6ft high mirror, two miniature models, two texts, raised platform with white circle and curtains, spectator as performer.

Photograph
Kerry Trengove

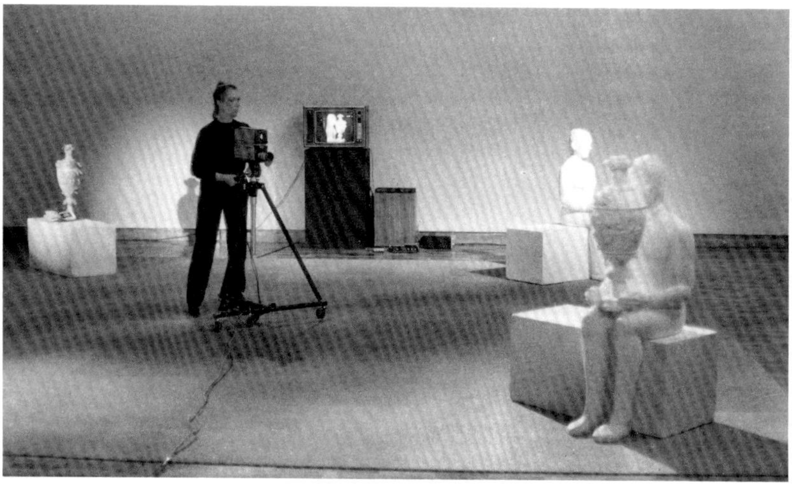

ART PRESS The performance began with a recording describing the waiting audience; but this description was in the past tense.The artist, pre-recording in the recent past anticipated the now/our present as already in the past. Simultaneously, we were, and we are looking back at the unfolding present from the future. To the question of reality and mimesis was added a complex perspective of layered time.

As the performance continued, the recording revealed that the book and vase were the ones used by the artist for a still life many years ago. Using a camera, the artist produced on the monitor a flat picture as nearly as possible identical in appearance to the original painting. At this point we heard her recall her exact feelings when working on the painting. Later, the mode of still-life was explored: to the art historian still-life is a genre which can be appreciated technically, culturally as form, and also culturally in terms of the complex of significance historically attached to the depicted objects. The artist as composer/image maker must be competent and conversant with cultural language. She knows the cultural significance of the objects: but their meanings to her are additionally loaded with contingencies of personal history and linked in her memory in ways which a painting could never reveal ... The real artist picked up each item in turn, took it to a figure, and sat so that momentarily her image on the monitor merged with her replica. Then the real was exchanged for the copy, and the copy put in place in the still life. Meanwhile, the memory of the items was told, adding layers of private and intense experience, and questions of reality proliferated.

Tam Giles, Primary Sources no 6, November 1980

Garrard took on both the role of Pandora and of the sculptor, enacting the role of subjection and ascribed culpability in counterpoint to the role of artist who seeks to carry her own history, and control her own image. The atmosphere of the piece, hushed and solemn, released a sense in the spectators that something was being ritually exorcised. The burden of Garrard's performance moved to affirmation and enablement for other women too, as she reworked patriarchal lore to incorporate it changed, into her personal mythology.

Marina Warner, 'Redressing the Balance', NGBK, Berlin, 1987

ART PRESS 'Beyond Still Life' (first performed as part of the women's exhibition 'About Time' at the ICA) was centred on a particular childhood occurrence – seeing her older brother kill a bird – that over-whelmed her capacity to express her feelings. In the tape accompanying the performance she says: "her anger will be seen as weakness ... she is afraid that any expression of her feelings will invite attack." Quietly she performed a compensatory gesture, placing the dead bird inside the house, next to a book and a vase which she was painting at the time, in an attempt to 'create a still life'. Memorial, act of transcendence, defusion, her desire for order becomes an archetypal act of feminine integration.

As counterpoint to this act of self-denial, interjected into the performance is a male voice reading the myth of Pandora "this first woman ... a heart filled with lies and cunning words ... brought pain and suffering to man." Pandora, woman as made by man, becomes the base of male cultural hegenomy. Thus counterpoised with the idea of self-denial in the personal narrative, Garrard's use of the Pandora myth functions as a metaphor for the colonisation of female creativity. Hence her integration into the performance as an object within a still-life – albeit that her role as performer is that of a manipulator of objects and co-ordinator of events – is a calculated attempt to position herself as a presence framed by the myth. What remains to be done, however, is to break down this frame-work; as she says in the text, it is necessary "to locate something beyond the still-life".

In this work Garrard is using her past as a source of fiction to be negotiated and transcended, an idea emphasised by the complementary use of myth. The myth of Pandora is not an arbitrary choice but a story avidly read and absorbed by the artist as a child; the recovery of the story determines a new reading, one that subverts and displaces the meanings formed by a younger self ... Garrard's transformation of incidents from her life into narratives of patriarchy is an insistence on the need for new stories, stories that hold the possibility of creating new languages, new forms, new roles. As she has said, "the role models have yet to be created for women by women".

John Roberts, 'Between Ourselves', Ikon Gallery, Birmingham, 1984

Photograph
Kerry Trengove

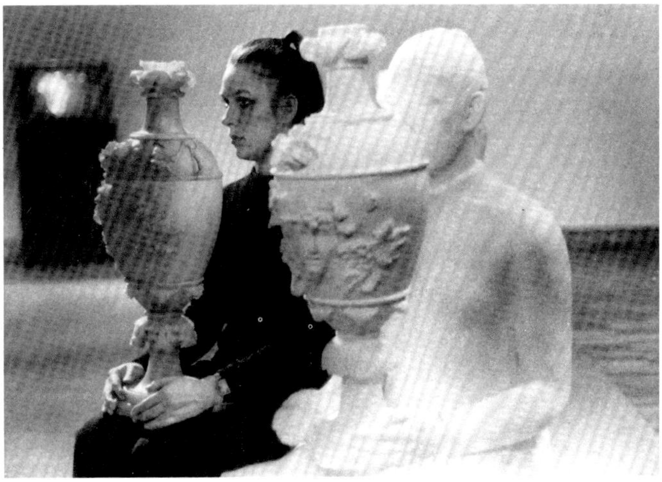

ARTIST'S NOTES 'The vase stands in its usual place on the piano, the light from the window glowing warmly through the alabaster head of a Greek god carved on its surface. Beside it lies a book, the pages opened at the myth of Pandora. A few inches to the left, between the vase and the book, the body of a small bird has been arranged.'

This apparently unimportant memory of the subject matter for one of my childhood paintings, forms the corner stone of my most recent work 'Beyond Still Life'. My relationship to objects has been central to the development of my own particularity as an artist. It has contributed to my present work placing itself beyond the six hundred year old, object-based history of European painting and sculpture. It has caused me to examine my role as an artist/object maker in relation to earlier art traditions and other cultures. It has caused me to question my role as a woman who 'turns herself into an object' (John Berger) and whose place in art history has been that of subject for, rather than creator of art. It has opened up a space for me beyond the objects that I make, in which these and many other questions become the content for my life work.

My childhood was peopled with a continuous stream of art, antiques and miscellaneous debris from diverse countries, periods and cultures. The house was over-filled with these 'things', bought for my mother's shop or made by my father who was a painter. To me each object seemed a silent key to history. Whatever its status or category in the world outside, each had its own integral meaning, value and power. My memory seems to recall only those objects directly related to incidents in family life. Examining this relationship between object and incident, past and present, cultural and personal history is the starting point for my art practice. 'It seems to spring from a minute and unimportant detail ... a starting point from which it invents lines, planes and a whole architecture ... the reader is beginning to get a glimpse of something.' (Allain Robbe-Grillet)

Whilst following the threads of this particular memory a spectrum of associations opens up, the vase, the book and the bird appearing in the historic genre of still life have a widely understood 'meaning'centred here on the myth of Pandora. This recognisable narrative element which they carry is explored in the work and gradually extended until through their private histories each becomes identified with cultural status, innocence, learning, creativity, skill, morality and gender. These paths of meaning cross at a common point, an apparently trivial incident in my distant past when my brother shot a sparrow. Recalling this small but traumatic event to which I remained a passive observer, led me to examine my detached 'still life' roles – the artist as observer, the passivity of the female model – and the role of active performer seen usually as a site of masculine power.

The 'unimportant' incident begins to take on other meanings, the prejudiced roles of these familiar stereotypes are questioned as the artist alternates between being performer, subject and spectator in relation to the objects. By looking beyond 'still life' into the surroundings, a matrix of meanings is gradually uncovered which link the trivial to the important, the personal to the universal, the everyday to the historic, the spectator to the performer.

Rose Garrard, 'About Time', ICA, London, 1980

SITES

'About Time' Institute of Contemporary Art London

Third Eye Centre Glasgow

COMPONENTS

First Pandora performance. Pre-recorded and live sound, central video camera on tripod, close-circuit to four monitors, four plinths with objects: the book, the vase, the bird and white plaster replicas. Three life size white seated figures. Artist performing in black clothing

CO-SELECTOR AND ORGANISER

'About Time' exhibition of time-based work by 21 women artists as part of Womens Images of Men series.

PREPARATORY DRAWING

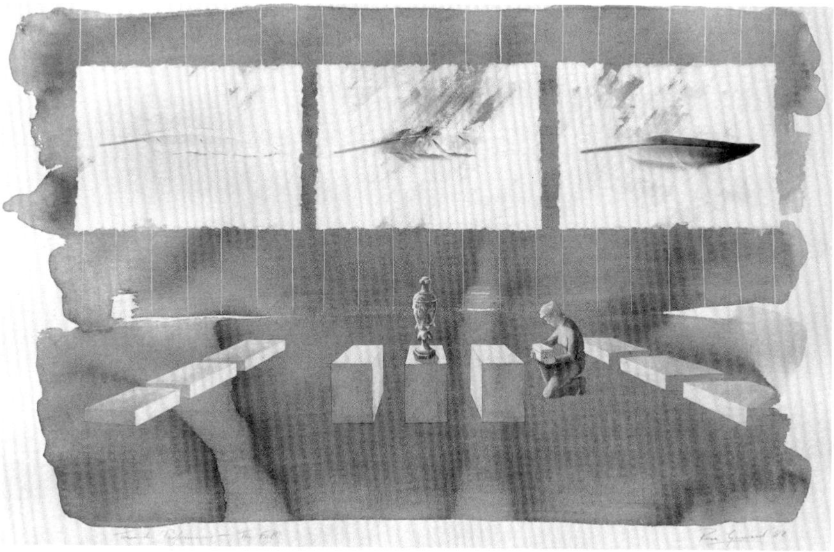

ARTIST'S NOTES The garden constantly reassessed, as territory, as enclosure, as defended space, as restriction, as internal space, as external landscape for contemplation and action. The experience. Memories each one smaller than the one before, until the personal becomes the universal. The particular, trivial, incidental, take on new significance. The garden, as source of knowledge, as paradise, as it is now, in the moment, the warmth, humidity, lightness, darkness, colour, sounds, silences, just being. The tape itself.
The garden planted, as symbol for the once virgin, as site of the fall from innocence, Eve's original sin, loving and leaving all that once delighted. The fall as flight, as flying from all that was nurtured. The fall from the planned future to uncertainty.
Rose Garrard 1980

Small Incident
Dog barking in the house
a brown bird falling
flying down.
Falling down
bolted down
some time singing
some time screaming.
Angry shouts in warm air.
It flew away
until tomorrow
it won't be there
Rose Garrard 1981

Red Rag
Seeing red
blood spilling the curse
from Pandora's vase
thicker than water
the fall
to Eve's apple
scarlet flight red handed
Rose Garrard 1982

ART PRESS 'The Fall' is concerned with the process of 'seeing', uncovering hidden meanings through the juxtaposition of personal and cultural histories and myths ... A matrix of journeys and connections are made; the Fall of Eve, the notion of Original Sin, Pandora's Box and the Bird of Hope, of victor and victim, of the mythological role of man and woman. In understanding the significance of these threads which make up this network of 'uncertain signs' (R. Barthes), the spectator, and his/her role becomes fused into the performance as the multiple concepts cohere and unfold.
Katy McLeod, Arnolfini Review, Bristol, May 1982

SITES

'Women Live' Arnolfini Bristol
'Women Live' London Film-Maker's Co-operative

COMPONENTS

Three large paintings with text on canvas stretched from white ropes, six plaster objects, six original objects, six interior lit boxes, close - circuit video and surveillance camera, two monitors. The artist performing in red clothing

COLLECTION

Preparatory drawing Victoria & Albert Museum London.

Absent Performer

1981/82

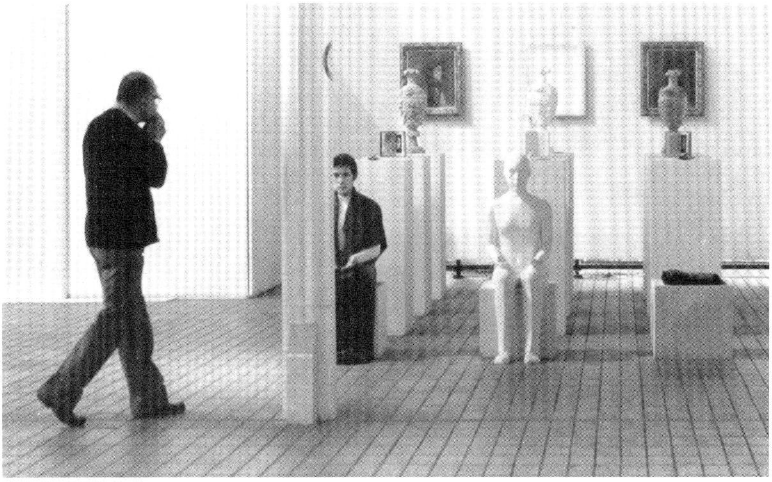

SITE

'Plastic Work by Performance Artists' ELAC Centre Lyon

COMPONENTS

Twelve four foot high plinths. Objects: the vase, the book, the bird; three original objects, three coloured replicas and three white replicas. Two life size figures and artists performance clothing folded on plinths.

Two Voices: White Feather

1981/82

ARTIST'S NOTES 'White Feather' centres around memories of the same childhood incident which has formed the core of several recent installation and performance works. Recalling this small but traumatic event, to which I remained a passive observer, led me to examine the detached role of the artist, watching, and the passive role of the female model, posing. These two stereotypes form an uncomfortable union within the mind of the single speaker, myself, resulting in two voices in two spaces the private interior (studio) and the public landscape (seashore).

Two voices, light and dark
two sides
of the same image.
Seeing with words
that hide what they are trying to reveal.
Two voices
speaking in parallel
along the same lines
parallel lines.
Between the lines
two voices
Artist and Model
in the same dark space
remembering an image
a white feather in a shaft of light.

Rose Garrard, 'Live to Air', Audio Arts, London, 1982

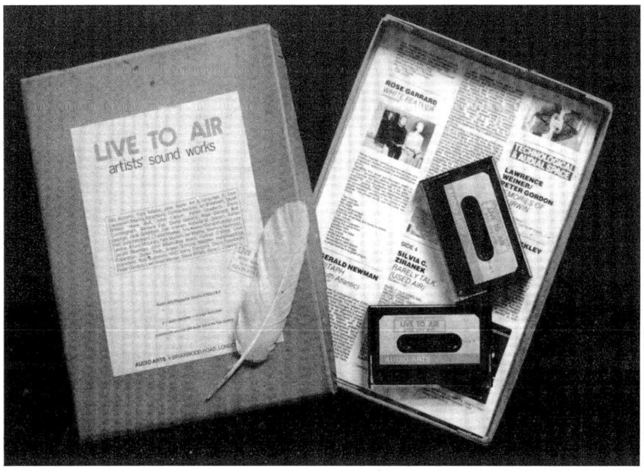

SITES

'Live to Air' Tate Gallery London and general distribution

COMPONENTS

Boxed audio cassette tape with catalogue

COMMISSION

William Furlong Audio Arts London .

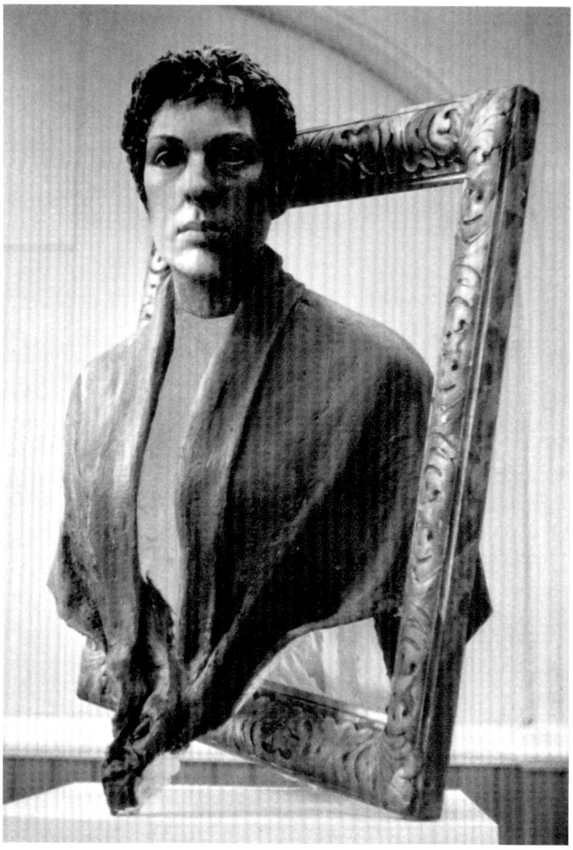

POPULAR PRESS Perhaps the prevailing mood of this memorable show is best summarised in the work called 'Artist as Model', where Garrard shows herself emerging from an ornate gold frame. She has managed to assume a solid, three-dimensional form, changing from a painted image to a sculptural alternative.

The transformation, however, is not complete. Part of her body still lingers within the frame and Garrard's sombre expression indicates that she entertains no illusions about the difficulties which today's women artists are bound to encounter in the future.

Richard Cork, Evening Standard, April 7 1983

ART PRESS Her deconstruction of stereotypes is always filtered through the re-construction of her past. For Garrard the idea of the re-presented image doesn't simply mark a loss – much of the current media-based work in America and Britain has been concerned with the lack inherent in the turnover of the stereotype and product image – but something regained, a sense of new beginnings. The re-presented image enters a more expanded relationship with its origins, something that was particularly evident in the exhibition 'Frameworks'

Garrard also literally puts herself 'in the picture' in a number of works. In 'Artist as Model' she again appears as the unknown model from 'Surveillance' but now emerging from the frame ... Garrard's work suggests a series of absences, of identity, of independence, of status, of power.

John Roberts 'Between Ourselves', Ikon Gallery, Birmingham 1984

SITES

Central Foundation School Bow London

'Frameworks' Lewis Johnstone Gallery London

'Frames of Mind' Kettle's Yard Cambridge

COMPONENTS

Life size painted plaster portrait and frame

COLLECTION

Contemporary Art Society London

RESIDENCY

Three months at Central Foundation School, Bow organised by Whitechapel Art Gallery with funding from ILEA.

Photograph
Edward Woodman

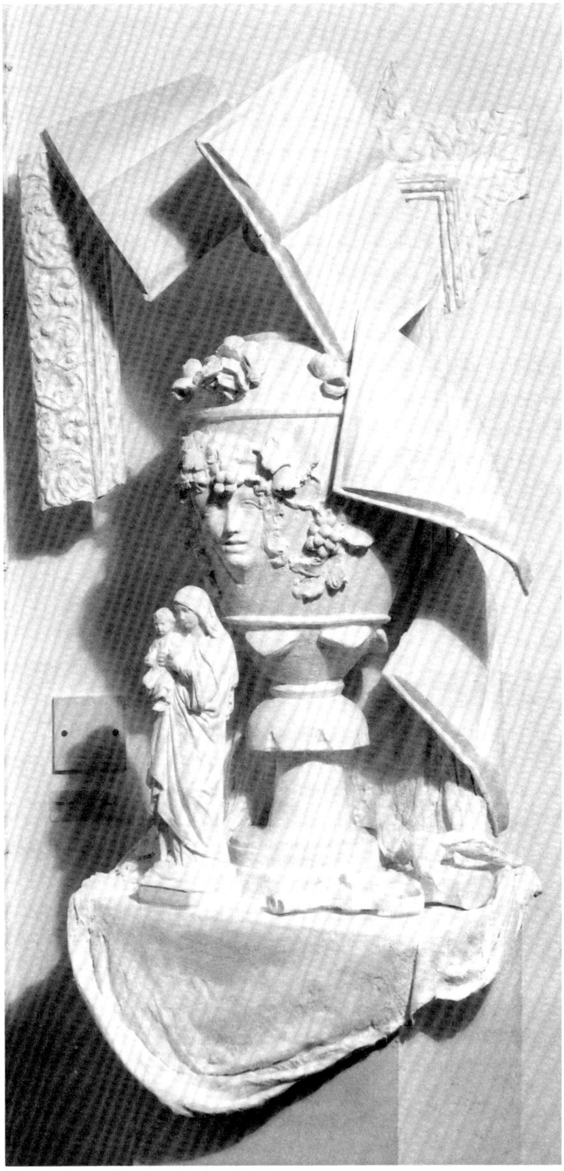

ART PRESS I think the whiteness has to do with notions of surface, of identity perhaps ... It came to be about erasing history and surface treatment, erasing the filters that hide what is, in an attempt to get back to the underlying form and see that for what it is. Whiteness keeps reappearing though, so there must be other reasons why I keep using it ... in the 'Beyond Still Life' performance it was as a re-evaluation of status and heirarchy through the use of the actual vase and a white replica.
Rose Garrard in conversation with Sue Arrowsmith 'Between Ourselves', Ikon Gallery, Birmingham, 1984

The myth of Pandora operates as an extension of, and a commentary on, the memory of the bird's shooting; the bird of hope left in the vase/casket becomes co-existent with the bird of personal narrative. Just as feminism, in its models of historiography, has informed post-structuralism (the emphasis on a synchronic reading of history) so Garrard's reclamation of incidents and objects moves across her past. Personal associations (a series of highly-charged events in her childhood and adolescence) re-emerge from the past to become the sites of conflicting ideas and emotions. Like any story-teller, Garrard re-writes her memory of events into dramatic form; objects take on the function of narrative signs, and as with most fictional transcription these events and objects are used for their general or universal qualities. This elaboration and commentary on the personal offers the possibility of entering the past on a productive level.
John Roberts, 'Between Ourselves', Ikon Gallery, Birmingham, 1984

SITES

Central Foundation School Bow London

'Frameworks' Lewis Johnstone Gallery London

'Frames of Mind' Kettle's Yard Cambridge

COMPONENTS

White plaster vase, books, bird, frame and drapery

RESIDENCY

Three months at Central Foundation School, Bow, organised by Whitechapel Art Gallery with funding from ILEA.

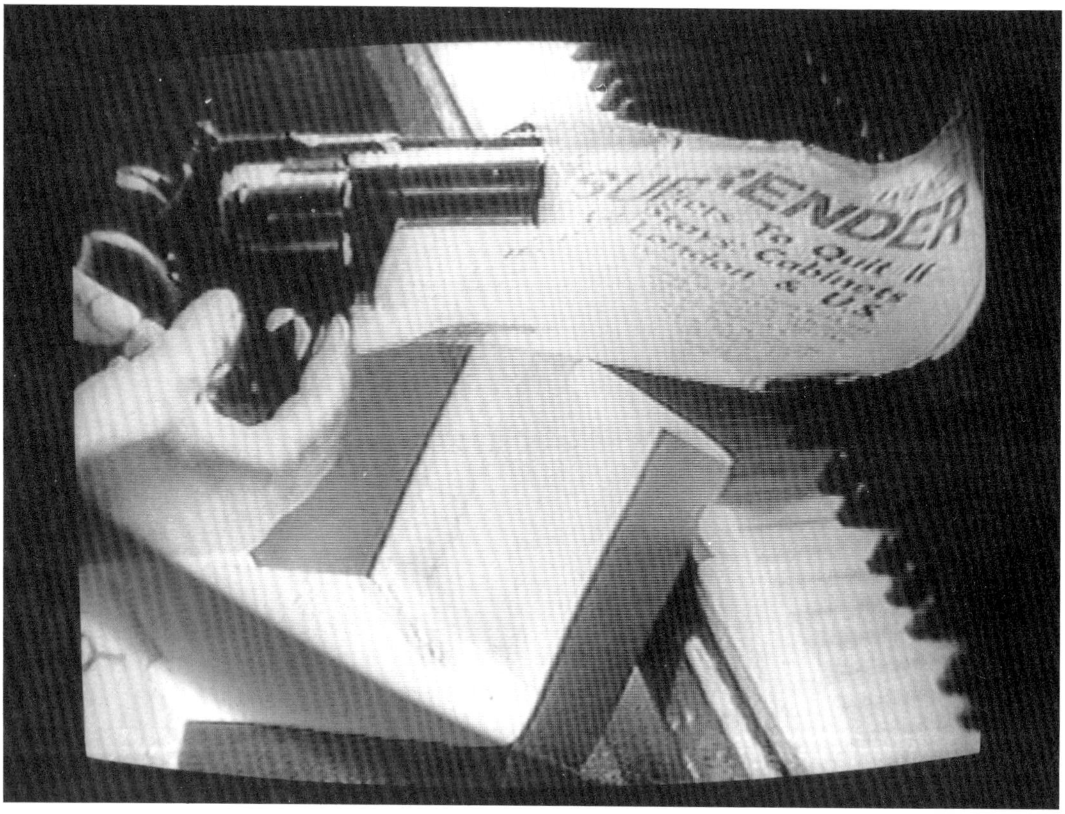

POPULAR PRESS She looked at the history of the school, at old albums of photographs, portraits and documents, and, coming upon an old Victorian chest of early Victorian accounts all neatly tied into little packets, she found herself confronting a long established obsession of her own with the story of Pandora and her Box. The metaphorical possibilities are endless, especially so in the context of a girl's school, with all the contradictory claims made upon them by education, expectation and conditioning ... It could all be seen as subversive perhaps, and therefore threatening, and so it is in a discretely feminist way, but there can be no Art where the mind is not touched, and the School, to its great credit has recognised that the statement is seriously considered and reasonable to make.
William Packer, Financial Times, December 1982

ARTIST'S NOTES The repetition is comforting ... inside the deserted institution ... empty corridors ... closed doors ... sounds, smells ... anticipated from an earlier time. Memories of childhood games ... stilled to silence with a glance. Conformity. Writing lines ... learning to conform. The repetition ... endless repetition ... endless formal lines ... rigid rows before the camera ... unsmiling faces ... uniforms.
For King and country ... for those who died ... Laid down her life ... endless names, listed.
Focusing on the chair, centre stage. The power symbol ... waiting for an occupant. The chair remains the same ... its position changes daily. Occupants come and go. Reading between the lines is terrifying.
Rose Garrard 1983

ART PRESS An extraordinarily prolific multi-media and performance artist, Rose Garrard has become one of the few of this type to get a measure of establishment support ... She is apparently at the peak of her powers, overflowing with energy, images and ideas.
... She is an Artist; one that performs, makes videos, takes photographs, makes sculpture, paints pictures and writes scripts in addition to working in a poetic vein. Happily barriers between subject areas are beginning to fall, and Garrard's work in the area of 'anti-labelling' has surely influenced some attitudes.
Liz Rideal, Performance, October 1984

SITES

'Whitechapel Open' Whitechapel Art Gallery London

Many other exhibitions and video festivals both here and abroad

COMPONENTS

Twenty five minute video, scripted, taped, performed and edited by the artist

COMMISSION

Whitechapel Art Gallery and the Old Girls Association Central Foundation School Bow London.

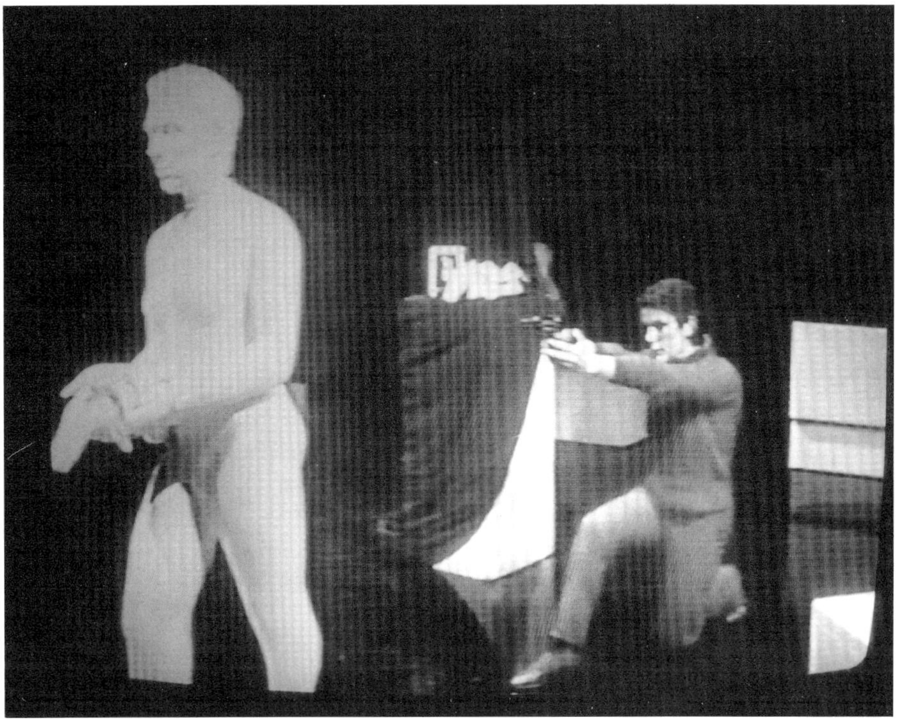

PRESS RELEASE Since the seventies Garrard's live performances have explored in various ways the power and prejudice of mythologies, particularly in relation to her dual role as artist and woman.

In 'Pandora, the Bringer of Gifts' earlier performances which examined the legend of Pandora were drawn upon to form the text of a new script for television. Now this narrative element appeared as part of a coherently visual structure scripted for the three studio cameras. The relationship between each camera and each of the three sculptural sections of the installation were planned to be revealed sequentially to the viewer, eventually showing the edge of the black 'set' within the white television studio. Garrard opens and examines both the contents of Pandora's mythical box, and the myths perpetuated by the illusions created on the 'box' of TV itself.

In this her first art work commissioned by television, she was allowed no editorial control, the series director editing the work back to a performance narrative. Though it retains only a little of its original structural concept, it remains a valuable record of her performance work at that time.

Anna Ridley, Annalogue TV Productions Ltd 1990

ART PRESS Each performer was offered three hours in the studio and a limited amount of time for preparation, and therefore had to have the works fairly closely scripted before shooting them. The series was called 'A Private View' (Director, Kevin Crooks: Associate Producer, Jonathan Harvey) and Garrard and [Stuart] Brisley both responded in interesting ways to tight schedules, adapting their own preoccupations to the rigorous studio lay-out. Neither programme had a spoken introduction, although captions which went up before each work offered brief information about the artist.

Garrard called her work 'Pandora the Bringer of Gifts'; using casts of herself as models, she performed alongside them, acting out the role of Pandora, bringing gifts. The text, sometimes spoken by Garrard in performance and sometimes in voice-over, narrated the story which often referred the viewer back to the roles of woman as artist, and as model. One was never allowed to rest in the fiction, being constantly drawn back from the illusion. 'Open it at the story of Pandora. Try to create an identical image. Try to adjust your position, remember the model in the book.'

Garrard's performance was meticulously planned and executed but still bore marks of television production through which the artist's work has been mediated. The studio layout, tracking of the camera and inevitable fades were fundamental to conventional televisual language and occasionally uncomplementary to the artist's intentions.

Tamara Krikorian, Art Monthly, February 1984

SITES

Television South West regional broadcast. Also widely shown in exhibitions and video festivals both here and abroad

COMPONENTS

First artist's work for television. Artists script and visual storyboard. Art objects as props, and artist as performer in red clothing

COMMISSION

Television South West series 'A Private View'.

Photograph
R J Boyle

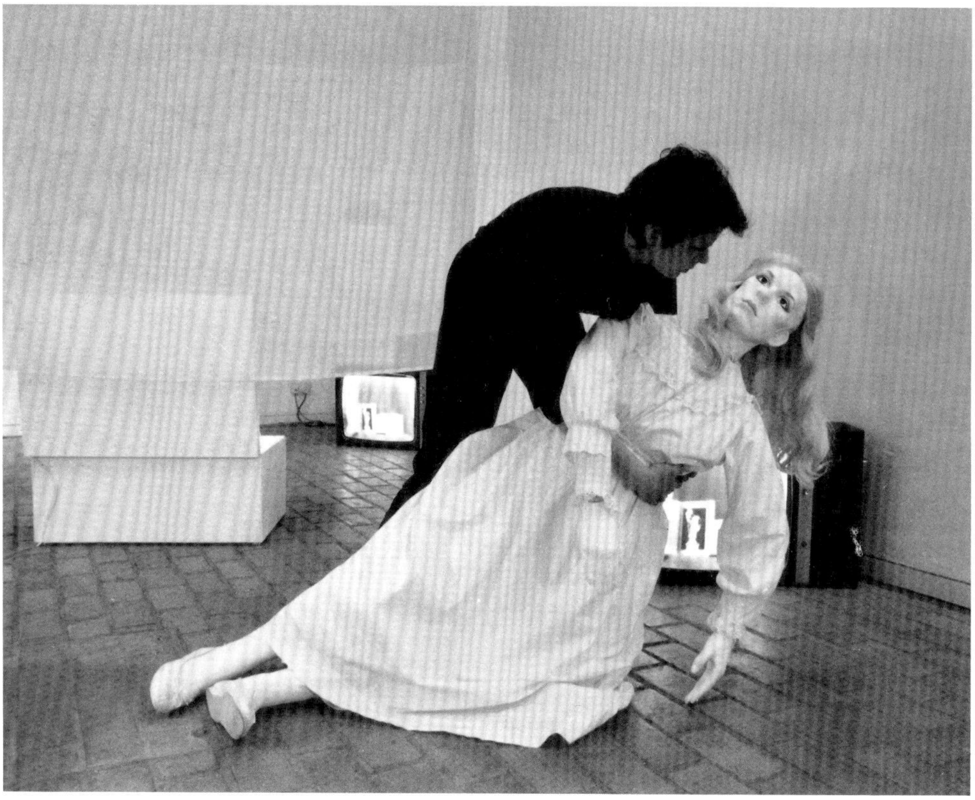

ART PRESS In 'Frames of Mind', the installation suggests and the performance explains the way that the Pandora myth and other symbols are entwined with Garrard's life. Most of us make emblems of our experience, it is a way of giving a sense and pattern to our fragmented lives. This is the implication of 'Frames of Mind', where actual objects (and her own body) are combined with different kinds of representation. Part of the power of symbols lies in their illusiveness. Like Garrard's works, symbols suggest, they offer possibilities, layers of meaning; they don't prescribe or define.

We can begin to trace Garrard's personal use of symbol by looking at the example of the bird. It may imply all sorts of meanings depending on what experience the viewer brings to it. Clearly in Garrard's work it tends to refer to the bird of hope which was left in Pandoras box. Sometimes the bird is dead, its legs upturned. As a child she watched her brother shoot a bird. This kind of personal significance applies to other images. We are told that a revolver belonged to her father, a statue of the Virgin to her mother, a vase like a classical urn was given to Garrard as a baby. Her work is cool and classical and it is at once steeped in, and comments on history, and examines the possibilities in life and art, for change and choice (for Eve and Pandora choice was a foregone conclusion). But its fascination lies in the way that ideas are embodied in associative visual images, and in the explanatory verbal and dramatic material which she has used to expand the limits of her art.

Caroline Collier, Artscribe, Spring 1983

ART PRESS Rose Garrard initially trained as a sculptor in Birmingham, London and Paris. The title 'sculptor' no longer seems appropriate; it is too confined and traditional for an artist whose investigations have been enriched by her work in television, theatre and magazines and who now successfully challenges the conventions of categorisation.

Ann Compton, 'Frames of Mind', Kettle's Yard, 1983

SITE

'Frames of Mind' Kettle's Yard Cambridge

COMPONENTS

Three light boxes, three suspended gauze screens, a slide tape sequence of images of Pandora, Joan of Arc, and the Virgin Mary. The original Pandora book, statuettes of Mary and Joan of Arc, and white replicas. A life size fibreglass 'doll'

Close-circuit video with surveillance camera and three monitors
Artist as performer in black clothing

A quantity of other individual art works from 1980 onwards.

Bolt Upright

1983

Photograph
Edward Woodman

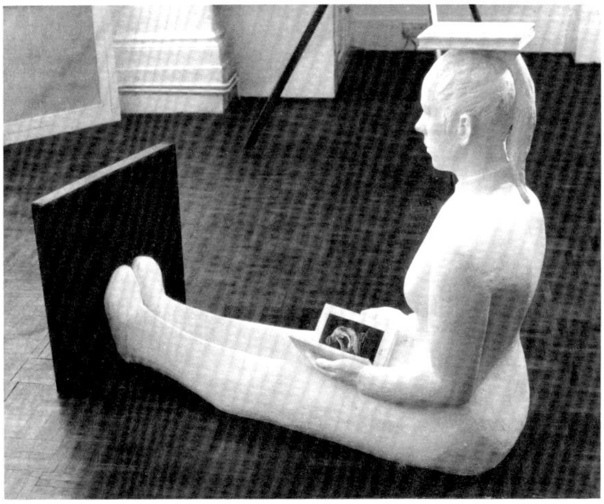

POPULAR PRESS Somewhere deep within the gleaming, all-obscuring whiteness of much of Rose Garrard's art, the public mythology becomes a private one. This exhibition is cluttered with plaster casts of objects from her past. As a girl she was given a book, Legends of Greece and Rome, in which the legend of Pandora was illustrated by a statue – an example of high Victorian perfection by Harry Bates, now in the Tate Gallery – which is the model for all Rose Garrard's Pandoras.
Waldemar Januszczak, The Guardian, March 9 1983

ART PRESS They're dependent on each other, the mould and the model. When you cast-up and get a replica of what is live, it's more the difference between the two, the live and the static that interests me. It's to do with the notion of duplicating, and derives in part from my experience of working with live models, taking casts from them, and in part from my fascination with the shell, with surface and mask. All the way through, my work has been about the hard lines that people draw around things. So when the soft model is wrapped by soft plaster and the plaster becomes hard, it becomes a shell, a protection, a container and restriction.

Virtually everything I've done, since about 1974, has been concerned with how categories of various kinds have been arrived at – whether history, art, or 'femininity' and how notions of 'good' and 'bad' have been arrived at, on a moral as well as cultural level.
Rose Garrard in conversation with Sue Arrowsmith, 'Between Ourselves', Ikon Gallery, Birmingham, 1984

SITES

'Frameworks' Lewis Johnstone Gallery London

'Self Expressed' Spacex Gallery Exeter

COMPONENTS

Steel and plaster, life size figure.

Pandora Rock Drill

1983

Photograph
E Hamilton-West

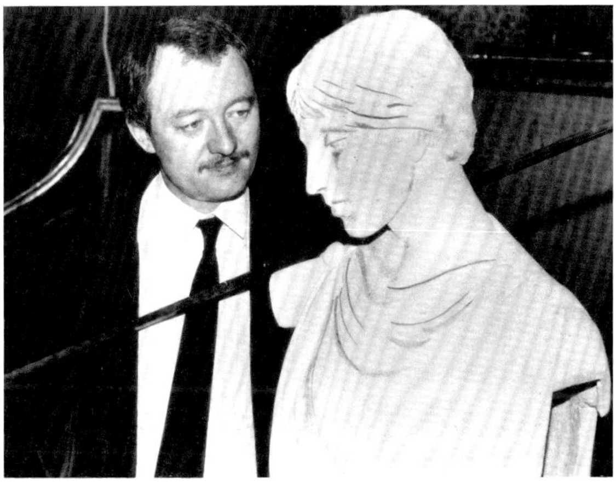

POPULAR PRESS The most direct of Rose Garrard's self portraits as Pandora is a modern version of Jacob Epstein's 'Rock Drill'. But where that First World War sculpture shuddered with all the aggressive, metallic, masculine energy of its times, Rose Garrard's Pandora is curled around the top of a tripod like a chiffon scarf. Her head and shoulders are based on a piece of Victorian statuary and, therefore, boast an impossible perfection. Another impossibility, Pandora's choice, is signified by the two birds on her shoulder, one black, the other as white as snow.
Waldemar Januszczak, The Guardian, March 9 1983

SITES

'Frameworks' Lewis Johnstone Gallery London

'Residency Exhibition' Birmingham City Museum and Art Gallery

COMPONENTS

Steel and plaster, life size figure.

Photograph
Edward Woodman

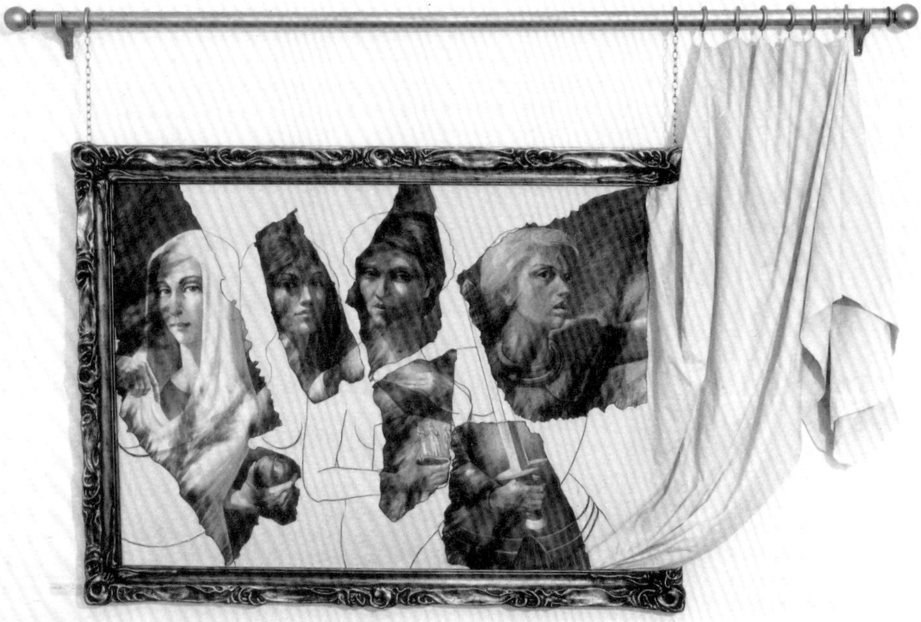

ARTIST'S NOTES My recent work is an exploration of the traditional relationships between the roles of the artist, the model, and the idea of the frame. The term artist has assumed a male gender, that of model has presupposed a female subject, and the idea of the frame, particularly a gilt frame, has been seen as elevating the status of the image.

In protecting and defining the subject, the frame also restricts the image, quietly limiting its meaning. In this exhibition, the power of the frame is part of the meaning of the work, acting as a metaphor of the unseen frameworks in which we are contained, and within which we contain ourselves. In some work the frame remains closed; in other work it is forced open, made to flow, evaded, transformed.

Within the frames, the models I have chosen derive from mythological, historical, and personal sources – the Virgin, Eve, Pandora, Joan of Arc, and Vigée-Le Brun, Gentileschi, Leyster and the anonymous model first performed by me in 'Surveillance'. The subjects have been chosen to initiate questions about the perpetuation of the image of the female model, about the limitations surrounding mythological and historical female archetypes, and about the invisibility of the women artists who could act as effective role models.

Part of the meaning of the work challenges the art historical assumption that women should be contained by the frame but rarely seen as creators of it. This intent extends to confronting other conventional categories – for example, the boundaries between painting and sculpture – in an attempt to open out habitual frames of reference. The individual works are not passive but determinedly active.

Rose Garrard, 'Frameworks', Lewis Johnstone Gallery, London 1983

ART PRESS This exhibition is about choice; the illusory element of choice in a decision to act, when such action has meaning only in terms of a pitifully small number of unattainable role models. Garrard's act of denial, which undermines the paradigmatic practices of 'risk-taking' and 'tackling major issues', is composed of a double moment. On the one hand she is stripping away so much metaphorical dead wood from her chosen symbols, revealing them, with clarity, in their own particular, factual existence. But at the same instant that these works seem to fall apart into the countless, disarticulated elements, the possibility of a far richer poetry becomes evident. What Garrard's work insists upon, is that to offer someone a choice is insufficient; what matters is that one must be offered the possibility of making that choice ... The offer to each of us of the responsibility which attends the search for meaning is one made in good faith; Pandora's and Garrard's Bird of Hope is an ever present companion.

Michael Archer, Art Monthly, April 1983

SITES

'Frameworks' Lewis Johnstone Gallery London

'Frames of Mind' Kettle's Yard Cambridge

'Between Ourselves' Ikon Gallery Birmingham

COMPONENTS

Canvas, calico, gilt frame, oil paint, and curtain rail .

Photograph
Edward Woodman

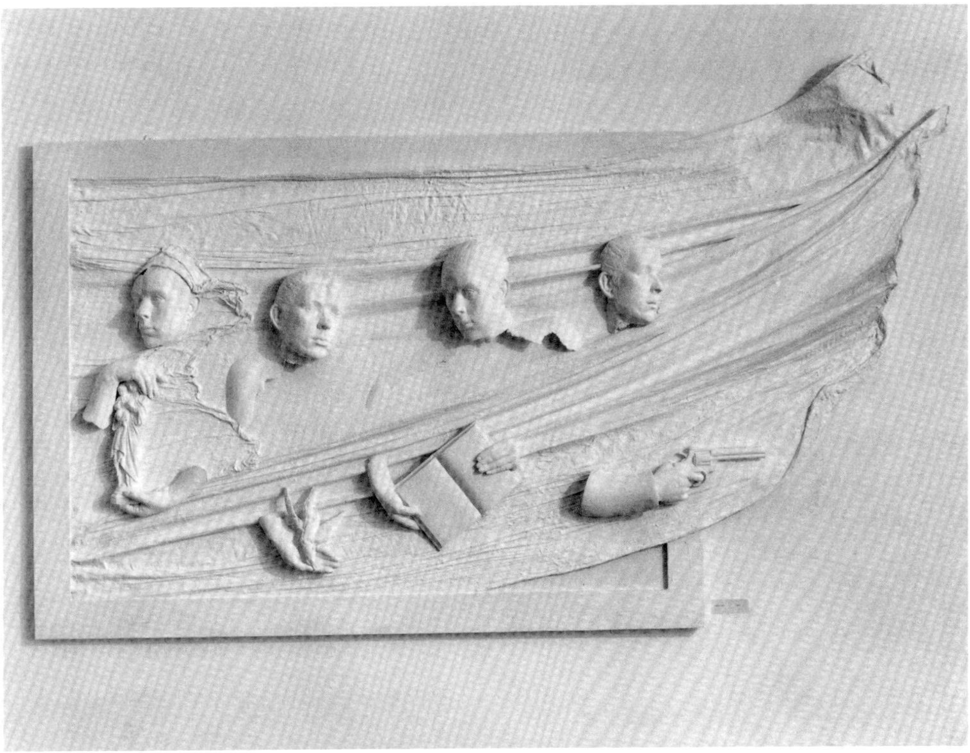

POPULAR PRESS 'Freeze Frame' is a frieze of plaster self-portraits in which Rose's head adopts the attitudes of the role models offered her as a child, her hands holding casts of symbolic objects. The Virgin holds a cast of the Madonna placed beside her bed by her Catholic mother. She offers a spiritual life that is determined by religious dogma and ruled by sexual constraint. Eve, holding the little bird, represents the passivity of the woman who sees herself as a powerless observer, one cowed into inertia through circumstance. This time Pandora opens a book, the container of knowledge and a possible way forward. Yet language is tailored to lend credence to the thoughts of men, while the knowledge available to us represents a masculine view of the world. Joan brandishes the gun, having adopted the active masculine role. But aggression represses women and therefore offers no real alternative. It's a gloomy set of options, but the backcloth of 'Freeze Frame' flows beyond the boundaries of the constraining rectangle, implying that growth and change are possible – choice is not altogether a myth.
Sarah Kent, Time Out, March 1993

ARTIST'S NOTES 'Freeze Frame' was an attempt to make visible the 'trauma of eventlessness' in the lives of women. To explain ... I'm in front of the camera and being recorded for television. The Director is instructing me to turn my head this way then that, to turn the book towards the camera, to bend my knee a bit more. Out of the corner of my eye I can see a video monitor with my image live on it. The image looks perfect. The Director is pleased. I'm pleased – my discomfort, my distortion for the viewer didn't show. It's only on the train home that it dawns on me that I've been fulfilling the classic role of the catch 22 female model, looking good at the expense of my own feelings, my reward was pleasure at 'his' pleasure. This is the moment when everything stops, when nothing changes, when gender conditioning freezes the frame. The next day I began work on 'Freeze Frame'.
Rose Garrard 1986

SITES

'Frameworks' Lewis Johnstone Gallery London

'Frames of Mind' Kettle's Yard Cambridge

'Between Ourselves' Ikon Gallery Birmingham

COMPONENTS

Pigmented resin and fibreglass panel.

Photograph
Edward Woodman

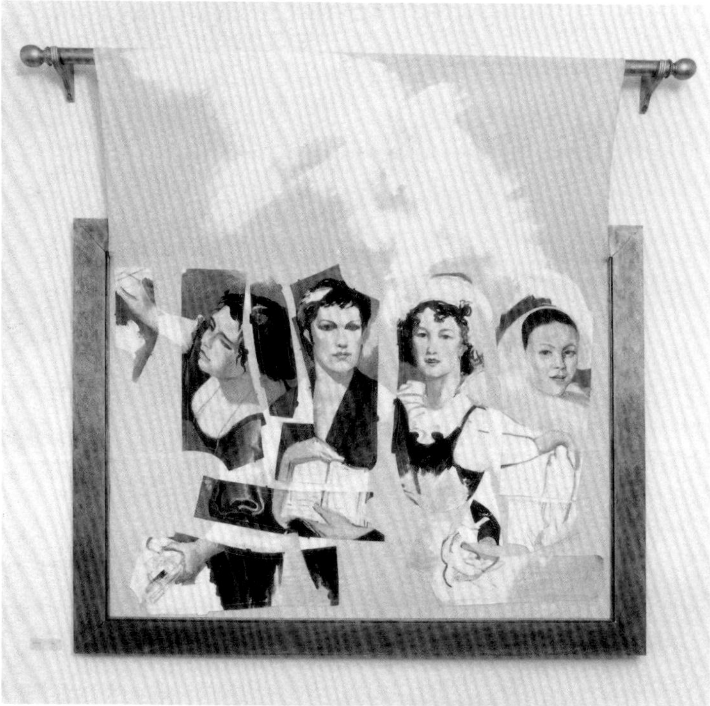

ART PRESS Four emblematic figures – Eve, Pandora, the Virgin Mary and Joan of Arc, haunt Rose Garrard's impressive and evocative exhibition at Cambridge ... A persistent image is the illustration (in the book where Garrard first read about Pandora) of Harry Bates's idealised, classical nude of Pandora. Garrard has made life size figures of this statue and of herself reading the book. There are semi-ironical references to domestic settings with paintings hung from curtain rails, references to the picture as a window and female images stuck and stitched, like the pattern for a dress.
Ideas are woven in a net of symbols and correspondences. As certain figures recur from piece to piece, painted, sculpted, cast and in relief, so do emblematic objects. Here then are a bird, a revolver, a book, a casket, statues of the Madonna and Child and Joan of Arc. These props all refer more or less directly to the four central figures of Garrard's iconography, which are, in some sense self portraits.
Caroline Collier, Artscribe, Spring 1983

Her work implies a woven continuum, and the protagonists and figures in the web are constantly being worked anew. Like Helen of Troy, who in the course of the Trojan War was weaving her own story at her loom, Garrard is fabricating a tale of which she is part and which will never be finished or fixed. This continuous patterning becomes both her stated theme and determines her methods. Exchanges take place between one piece and another, they communicate to the viewer the process over time during which they came into being, and so the installations and objects are continuously evolving in response to inner experiences as well as outer circumstances.
Marina Warner, 'Redressing the Balance', NGBK, Berlin, 1987

SITES

'Frameworks' Lewis Johnstone Gallery London
'Frames of Mind' Kettle's Yard Cambridge
'Between Ourselves' Ikon Gallery Birmingham

COMPONENTS

Canvas, calico, gilt frame, acrylic paint, roller blind.

Photograph Whitechapel Art Gallery

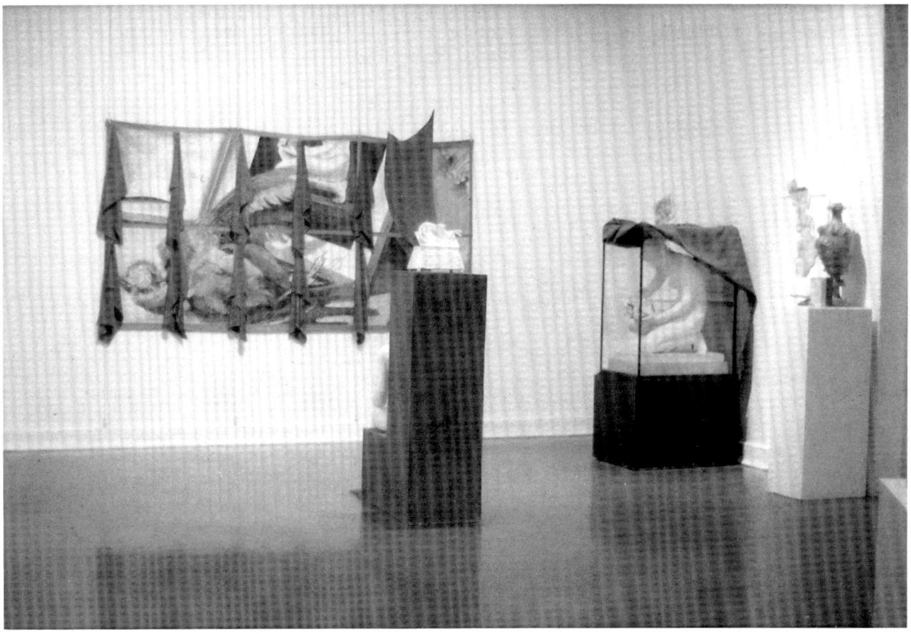

POPULAR PRESS Pandora is the focus of her Whitechapel installation watched over by Harry Bates' sculpture of Pandora, normally stashed in the basement of the Tate. When Pandora opened the infamous box, out poured all the disasters that beset mankind - plague, famine, pestilence, the lot. Only the bird of Hope stayed behind to offer a glimmer of salvation. The message from the patriarchs who created the myth is clear. Women must not be allowed to get their hands on knowledge - enquiry must remain the preserve of men. Or to put it more bluntly, an informed woman is a threat.
Sarah Kent, Time Out, March 25 1983

ARTIST'S NOTES Some months before this exhibition I had visited the 'Live to Air' show at the Tate to hear my audio work 'Two voices; White Feather' and in the bookshop discovered a postcard of the 'Pandora' figure which I had only known from a childhood book of Greek Myths and Legends. On enquiring I was told the sculpture had been in their basement store since being purchased for the collection in 1891. I made an appointment and a week later was led through long underground corridors lined with art to meet her. As until then I had only seen one photograph of 'Pandora' and I had no idea whether she was actually the size of an ornament or a monument. A dust cover was lifted to reveal a beautifully carved life size figure in white marble still under its original Victorian glass case. She was holding a casket of bronze and ivory which ironically was the reason she had never been moved, conservators fearing that her unsupported arms would break under its weight. The Whitechapel Art Gallery undertook complex and lengthy negotiations to borrow her for my installation, resulting in 'Pandora' finally appearing here, in public for the first time this century. Afterwards she remained on display at the Tate, and soon influenced another artist Hans Haacke who included her image as an ornament in his portrait of Margaret Thatcher.
Rose Garrard 1994

SITE

'Whitechapel Open' Whitechapel Art Gallery London

COMPONENTS

Life size white plaster figure with replica of my father's box, actual box, and replica of Bates' Pandora's box. Large painted canvas of book, and the original Harry Bates' 'Pandora' (exhibited first in 1891) lent by the Tate Gallery London.

Flaccid Guns

Photograph
Edward Woodman

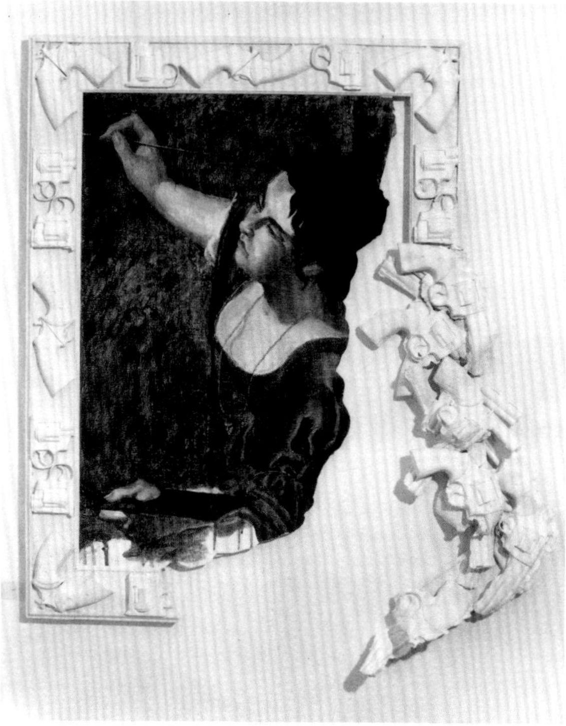

POPULAR PRESS A self-portrait by Artemisia Gentileschi repainted as a fresco on plaster and framed by gun fragments – Rose Garrard's 'Flaccid Guns' carries a wealth of personal and public references. Guns, symbols of destructive macho virility, have a special meaning for her. As a child she was forbidden to open the box containing her father's service gun. Later he left it to her in his will.

The box opens, the frame crumbles – women, traditionally the passive subjects of men's art, recreate their own images. The controlling power of the gun, the frame, is broken. If Gentileschi represents 'fallen woman', the painter Judith Leyster symbolises the virgin who also transcends social norms by picking up the brush. Her self portrait is framed by cascading Madonnas cast from the virgin placed by Rose's bed by her Catholic mother.

Sarah Kent, Time Out, March 25 1983

In many of the exhibits the dominance of the frame is contested and partially broken down. Several paintings are based on self-portraits of women artists from the past and in each case they turn out to be distinguished painters who suffered great indignities.

Artemisia Gentileschi, the 17th century Italian artist, was raped by a ruthless friend of her father's. Judith Leyster, at work in Holland during the same period, was almost erased from history after her death by dealers who attributed her work to male contemporaries like Hals. And Elizabeth Vigée-Le Brun was exploited both by her step-father and the man she was forced to marry, handing over the payments received for her portraits in order to absorb their debts.

Ultimately all three women triumphed over adversity; Gentileschi channelled her aggrieved fury into marvellously combative paintings of Judith beheading Holofernes, while Vigée-Le Brun became a successful and prolific painter much favoured by Marie Antoinette. Even the neglected Leyster is coming into her own now that wrongly ascribed canvases have been restored to her authorship and Garrard's images reflect the idea of resisting the limits which society has placed around women artists.

Frames refuse to travel all the way round pictures, breaking off in order to plunge towards the ground. Even when they do remain firmly fixed to all four edges of a painting, as in the portrait of Gentileschi, defiance is implied by the gun motif incorporated in the frame's decoration. But there is no sense of a battle easily won. Garrard's approach remains cool, analytical and tinged with a melancholy which acknowledges how much has yet to be done before women shake off all their constraints.

Richard Cork, Evening Standard, April 7 1983

ARTIST'S NOTES In the centre of the exhibition, suddenly I had this realisation that I had never experienced this situation before – of being totally surrounded by brushmarks by women artists that stretched right back through history. I felt part of a continuum for the first time. And there was anger, rage that for so many years there had been this absence that I couldn't even identify until now.

When I got back to London I had this sense that I really wanted to know this painting, (La Pittura by Artemisia Gentileschi) so I went to the studio without knowing what I was going to do, other than wanting instinctively to replicate the painting, to touch the image with my own brushmarks. I poured this plaster panel; I wanted a ground that flowed, that had movement and wasn't geometrically confined. It was reinforced with layers of scrim deliberately placed very close to the surface to break through it in places, so that the paint itself couldn't be totally controlled. So I began painting this fresco panel, hoping the acrylic paint would be absorbed differently by the two materials, sometimes resting on the surface, sometimes sinking into separate layers. I built the frame in plaster enclosing the image on three sides. This was the more measured intellectual response to the emotional need to reclaim the image, to absorb it into my own background.

Rose Garrard 1985

FLACCID GUNS, BIRD TALK AND MADONNA CASCADE

Photograph
Tate Gallery London

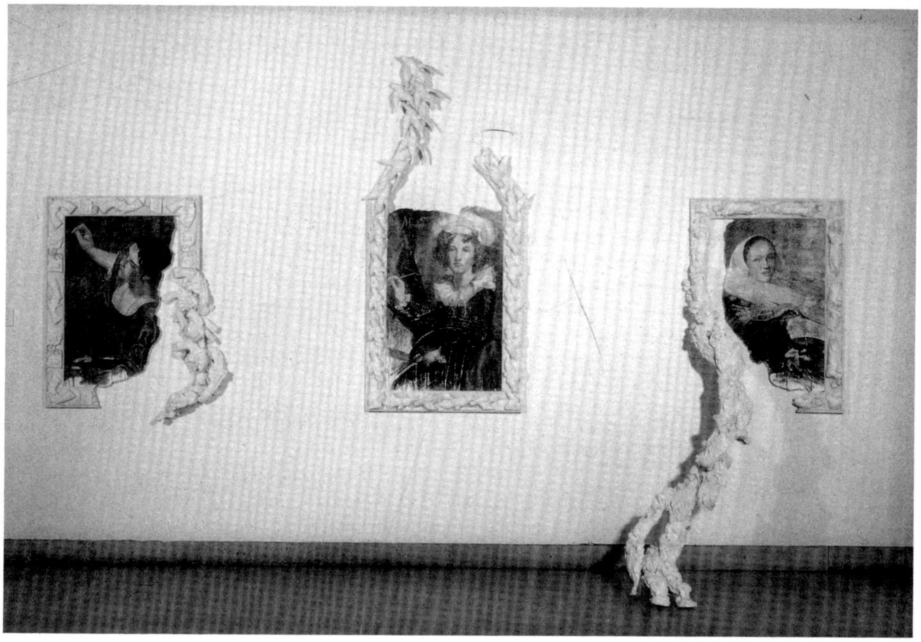

ART PRESS A series of paintings on plaster, based on portraits by once famous women artists, reveals that women have often chosen to become not only artists but their own models, a fusion of the active and passive roles. In these works the subject cannot be divorced from the surrounding frame which Garrard has constructed with casts of objects from her own childhood. The equally difficult male and female stereotypes, macho virility and virginal purity are summed up as impossible roles through the emblems of her father's service revolver and her mother's statue of the Madonna which tumble from the opened frames.
Ann Compton, 'Frames of Mind', Kettle's Yard, Cambridge 1983

The acrylic on plaster paintings have been combined with ornate plaster on wood frames of archetypal objects, but the frames dramatically open rather than enclose. In that of Gentileschi 'Flaccid Guns' the guns melt, flowing away from the image; in that of Vigée-Le Brun 'Bird Talk' the birds lift off from the image; in that of Leyster 'Madonna Cascade' the figurines tumble out to the floor. Garrard's reclamation of these artists may be an attempt to displace the aura and linearity of a male-defined tradition, but she is not interested in replacing this with any equivalent female pantheon. What interests her is the status these three women artists achieved in their time, their professional status as such. The recovery of these artists began in the early seventies, but for Garrard the question of unpacking the reasons why they were lost to history is not just an anthropological gesture, rather it cuts deep into her background and experience.
John Roberts, 'Between Ourselves', Ikon Gallery, Birmingham, 1984

ARTIST'S NOTES 'Models Triptych' was selected to be shown in 'New Art' at the Tate Gallery, an exhibition which claimed to show a range of the best work produced world-wide in the last four years. To me their inclusion signified the gallery's interest in representing women artists and I was thrilled that the images of these three self portraits which encompass a large part of our forgotten history, should appear in a mainstream exhibition reminding people of this absence. However when I looked around the exhibition I was disheartened to find that only six of the eighty four artists selected were women, and two of these appeared as partners of male exhibitors.
Rose Garrard 1987

POPULAR PRESS The masterpieces of a ghostly, ethereal, enticing exhibition are the series of pictures based on self-portraits by other women artists – other Pandoras. There's Judith Leyster, a serious and compassionate artist forced to make a living out of painting drunkards in the manner of her teacher, Frans Hals. The tempestuous Artemisia Gentileschi who was raped by her teacher and responded by making Judith Cutting Off The Head of Holofernes her favourite subject. The last but one of the female artists in the set is Elizabeth Vigée-Le Brun, a friend to Marie Antoinette and another plaything of the rococo.
Waldemar Januszczak, The Guardian, March 9 1983

SITES

'Frameworks' Lewis Johnstone Gallery London

'New Art' Tate Gallery London

COMPONENTS

Three plaster on wood, painted fresco panels with integral plaster 'frames'

COLLECTION

'Flaccid Guns' Alex Lotocki-de-Veligost New York

'Madonna Cascade' New Hall College Cambridge

'Bird Talk' Roger and Cathy Wills Cheshire.

Madonna Cascade

Photograph
Edward Woodman

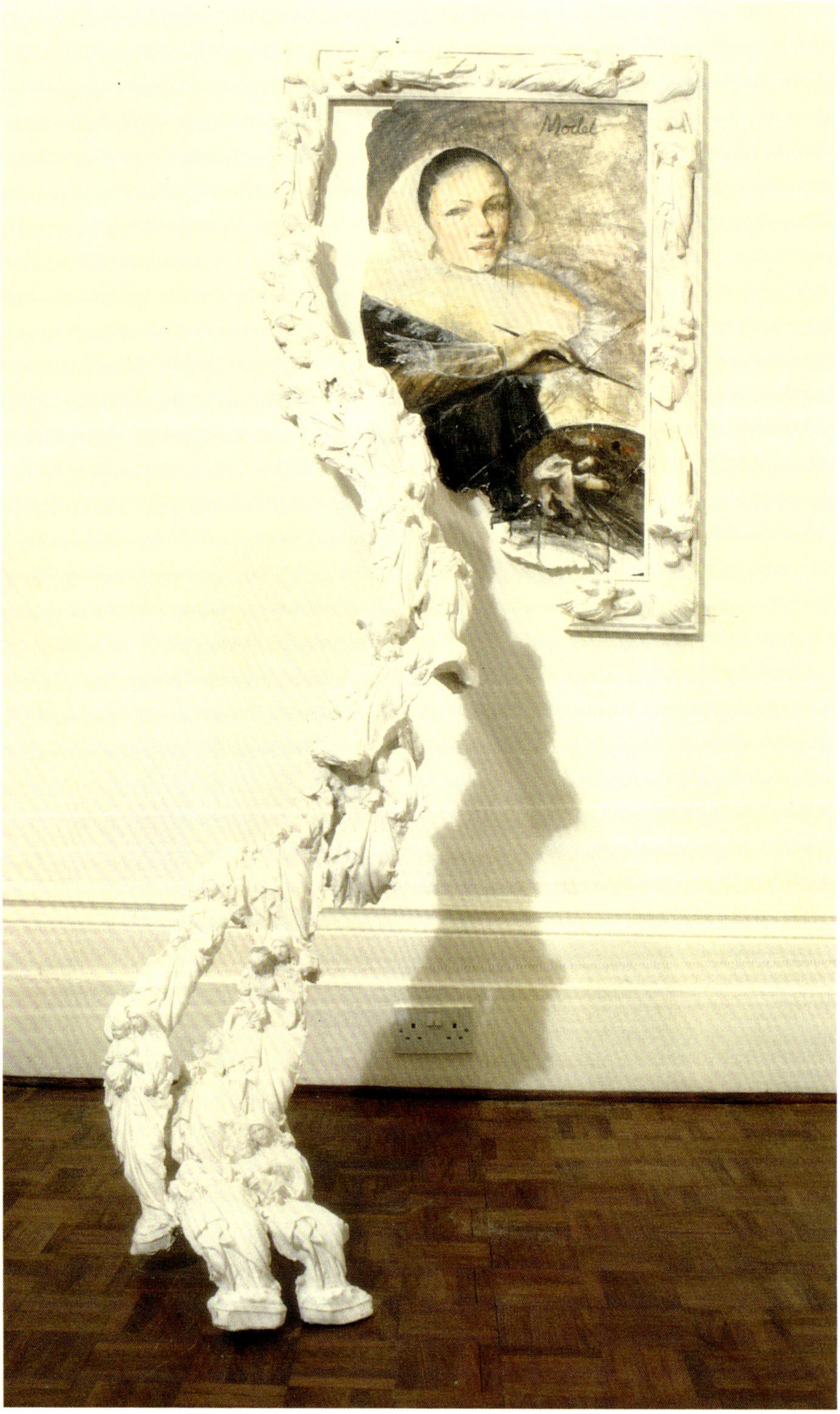

Window; Reclaim Kate Bunce

Photograph
Edward Woodman

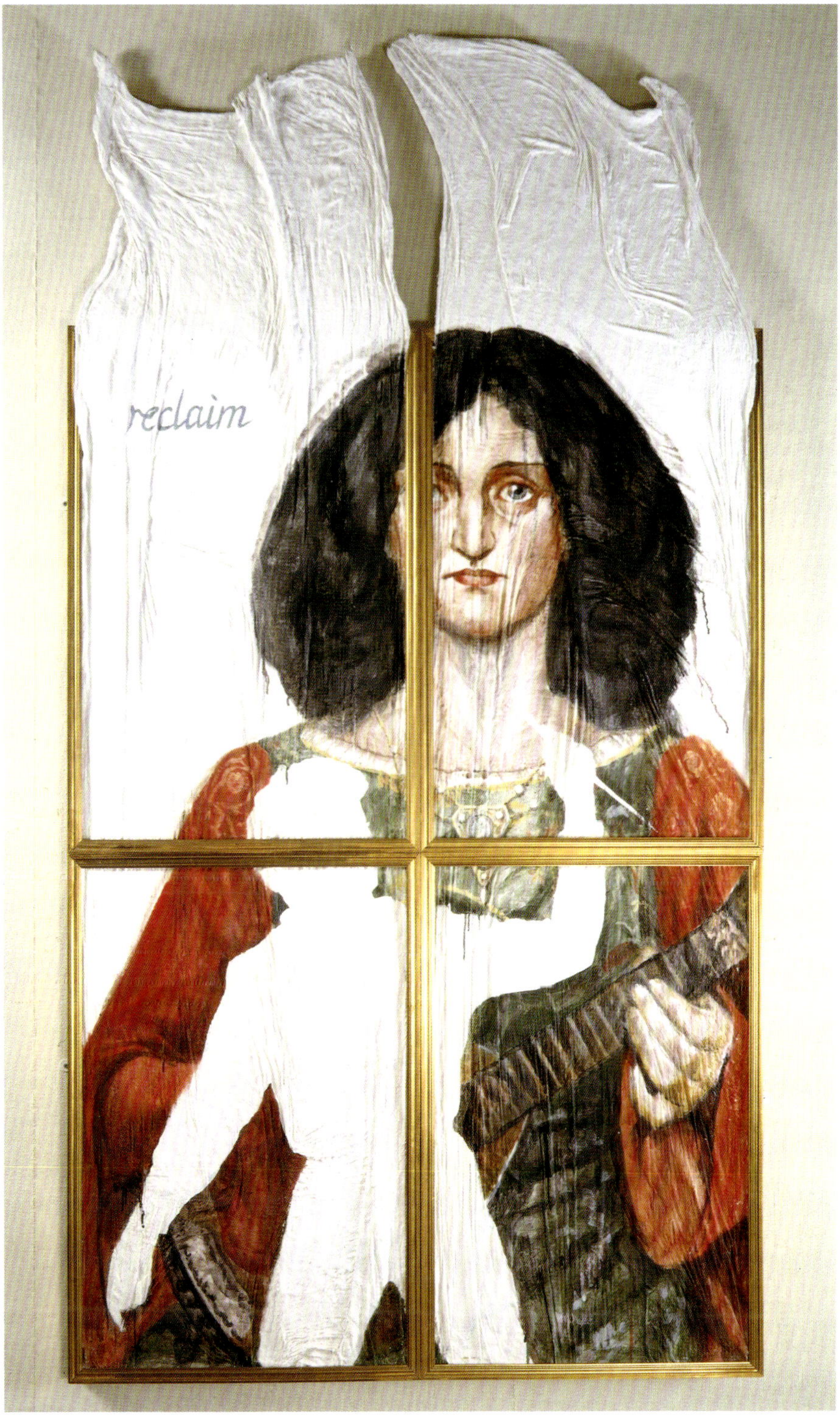

BEDSPREAD

Photograph
Ikon Gallery
Birmingham

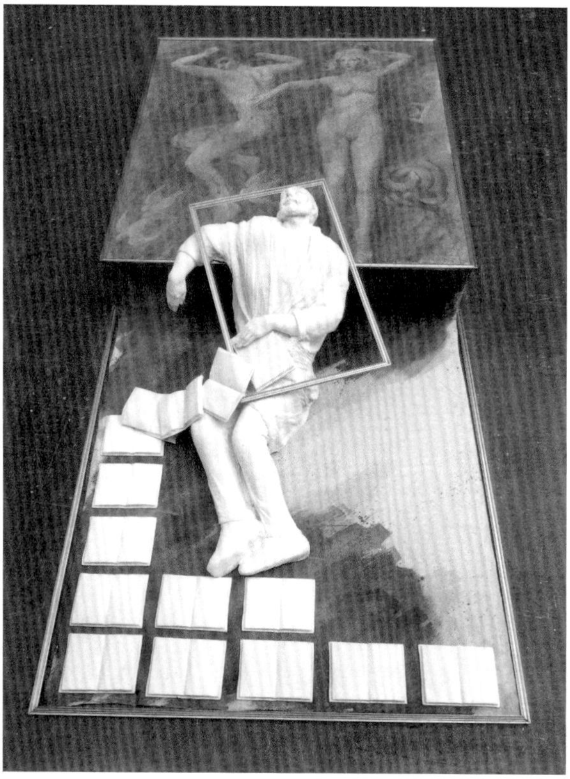

POPULAR PRESS From this position of the knowing woman artist Rose Garrard comments upon male/female relations. In her installation, the pieces 'Bed Spread' and 'Bed Head', two full-size plaster beds face each other across the gallery. Something about the distance they keep tells you that one belongs to a woman and the other to a man.

Lying in the first bed, awake, nervous, a gun under her pillow, is Degas' old beggar woman. She is unpainted, unadorned, Rose Garrard's standard symbol for reality. Slumped at the foot of another bed, drunk perhaps, for the book he was reading has slipped to the floor, is Joseph from Gentileschi's Flight into Egypt. This distance between the two beds, the two characters from art, says the artist is the real distance between an old man and an old woman. The unreal version, art's version, is preserved in a full colour image woven into the fabric of Joseph's bedspread. A perfect young Adam has found himself a perfect young Eve complete with snake and apple. On this hard contrast between the tired, worried face of Degas's old beggar woman and the erotic fantasy of Joseph's bedspread, this most impressive exhibition rests its case.

Waldemar Januszczak, The Guardian, February 1 1984

ART PRESS The predominantly white installation suggests the possibility of new beginnings within an elaborate web of personal and historical references. Along the main wall, a series of Window-pieces re-construct six idealised female portraits from the Birmingham collection as large, painted plaster reliefs, with the silhouette of the artist herself as an active participant in the reclaiming process. On each of the pieces, loose fabric-plaster moves outside the framework, evidence of new possibilities and choices beyond the stereotype ... The female is no longer considered in isolation and in this lies the central theme of the exhibition, as seen in two key works. In 'Bed Head', an old woman alone in bed holds a gun, an easily recognisable image of the female condition, which the artist links to the mythological idea of the Holy Family as portrayed in Orazio Gentileschi's (Artemisia's father) 'Rest on the Flight into Egypt' represented above her head. In 'Bed Spread', the book of knowledge that tumbles from the hands of a sleeping male figure is interpreted as the source behind a painted fantasy of Adam and Eve, the male-mythologized symbol of sexual relationships. In both these works Rose Garrard seems to have gone beyond specific personal or historical references, and has begun to communicate some of the searching and difficult issues that lie between male and female relationships.

Tessa Sidey, Arts Review, February 1984

Photograph
Ikon Gallery
Birmingham

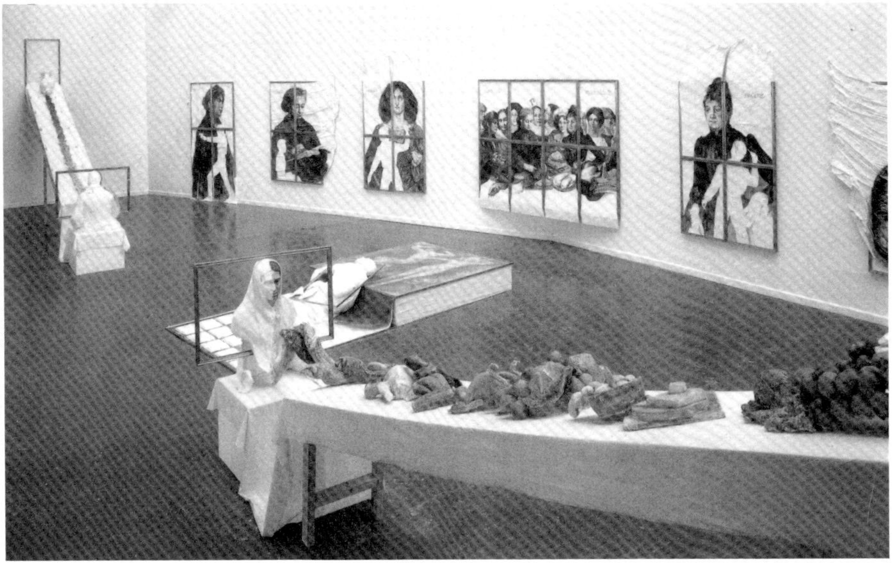

POPULAR PRESS Miss Garrard is a striking looking woman in her late thirties with the kind of facial bone structure that invites a portrait ... Her models are chickens, parsnips or cabbages. The inspiration is a picture she came across in the art gallery of a domestic interior. It is a handsome picture with a buxom cook surrounded by good things.

"It might be a symbolic representation of death in life" says Miss Garrard gesturing toward the fish and poultry. "But the mystery intrigues me since the picture may well have been painted by a woman."

When her creation is finished she will place a life sized female figure on one side of the banquet and a male on the other. At the moment she has cast a chicken in plaster and some vegetables and they resemble those remarkable things you used to see in fridges in gas and electricity showrooms.

Richard Edmonds, Birmingham Post, December 5 1983

ART PRESS In recent years Rose Garrard has questioned the hierarchies within art, and challenged the archetypal roles that surround women. She now develops these themes further in a three month residency at Birmingham City Museum and Art Gallery. Most of the new work in the current exhibition was produced during this period and, not surprisingly, makes direct references to the works in the Birmingham collection. The result is an absorbing insight into an artist reinterpreting and re-assessing existing works of art ... A sixteenth century Dutch painting 'Preparation for a Feast' provides the starting point for the optimistic wallpiece, 'Regenerate/Reconstitute', thirteen women gather to prepare a meal. The Last Supper theme is continued in two sloping tables that project down from either side of the installation space towards the floor. In 'Tilted Table; Cornucopia' a colourful, carefully prepared table of food slides down from an overturned classical urn towards a passive old woman, while on the other 'Tilted Table; Last Supper' a stream of red-tainted Madonnas move towards an equivalent old man; traditional symbols literally in the process of being re-evaluated.

Tessa Sidey, Arts Review, February 1984

ARTIST'S NOTES I want to re-work, re-establish, re-discover, re-appropriate, re-constitute, re-create ... I want to find ways of using and creating images of women and men that express the understanding of women and their fantasies...I hope one day to be in a position where I know that the work is not only being understood as coming from this female sensibility but is being valued equally to work by male artists.

Rose Garrard, press release, Ikon Gallery, Birmingham, 1983

SITES

'Between Ourselves' Ikon Gallery Birmingham &

Bluecoat Gallery Liverpool

Rochdale Art Gallery Lancashire

Midland Group Nottingham

Arnolfini Bristol

South Hill Park Bracknell

ICA London

COMPONENTS

Eleven large multi-media works

RESIDENCY

Artists Residency at Birmingham City Museum and Art Gallery, organised by Ikon Gallery Birmingham and funded by Arts Council of Great Britain and West Midland Arts. Source material; historic paintings in the collection of Birmingham City Museum and Art Gallery

COLLECTION

Window Series: Re-create, Harvey and Carole Lisberg Palm Springs California

Preparatory drawings, Birmingham City Museum and Art Gallery and many private collections.

Still from Video

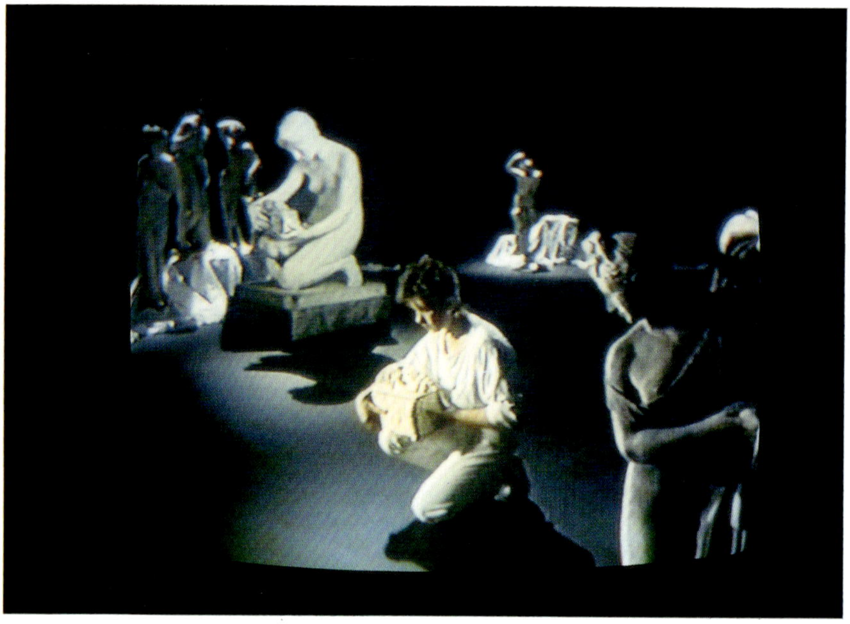

ART PRESS On this journey of discovery Rose Garrard takes the viewer in search of 'who we might become' through exploration of some existing female role-models. From the Television Studio we not only pass through the frame which surrounds the TV image itself, but through the gilt picture frame enclosing the passive artist's model to the psychological 'frames' of mind which affect our way of seeing or being womankind. This voyage through women from history and mythology, through situations from memory, fantasy, visualises the difficulties women face in moving beyond the restricted roles these figures have traditionally perpetuated. Moving down corridors of power and penetrating the crumbling cultural facade, reveals the original model of Pandora opening her box and causing the downfall of man, and the model of the Virgin Mother whose sexual purity is impossible to emulate. By appearing as Marilyn Monroe and Judy Garland the artist expresses the inner stress of these limited roles and the feelings of inadequacy behind the idealised image which may have contributed to these women's deaths. Hope is glimpsed as women artists from the past emerge briefly from the darkness, posing as their own models, and when the more positive aspects of Pandora as 'the perfect fusion of all things' are recovered in a reworking of the Pandora Myth. Meanwhile ... back in the studio, having the power to control the female image shifts continually between camera-man, artist, model, and the disembodied voice of the female producer.
Anna Ridley, press release, Annalogue TV Productions Ltd 1985

A woman is a woman is a woman – to paraphrase Gertrude Stein once again to the point and for obvious reasons – but the reality of womanhood is totally different from the symbolic representations of woman in art history. The images of women offered to us, such as the Madonna, Pandora, Judy Garland and Monroe, have acquired their weight through the artist's approach, through what he wants (or wanted) to express via/in woman. In an attempt to escape from this confined image and to meet the need to give it a new and more personal weight, the woman artist – in this case Rose Garrard – takes over the role of the models. She feels ill at ease in this strait jacket and the craving for a wider range of alternatives becomes steadily more acute. No innocent Madonna, no sex symbol designed merely for pleasure, but the mythic weight of Pandora provides a key: she denied humanity its gift of paradise, but endowed it with a more realistic world instead.
SB Women's Video Festival, Dortmund, Germany

With reference to mythology and history, Garrard's video is a critical survey of the social representations of women. Garrard offers a brilliant reworking of the misogynous myth of Pandora and examines the modern context which gave rise to the self-destructive idols – Monroe and Garland. Television screens are used as reframing devices to suggest a psychological 'frame' of mind that also limits perception.
Montreal Festival of Women's Film and Video catalogue, June 1987

SITES

Broadcast nationally on Channel 4 Television, shown widely at Video Festivals both here and abroad

COMPONENTS

24 minute video tape with sound, written and performed by the artist and others. Produced by Anna Ridley

COMMISSION

Artist's work for Channel 4 Television with Annalogue TV Productions Ltd.

Tumbled Frame II

Photograph
Barbara Beck

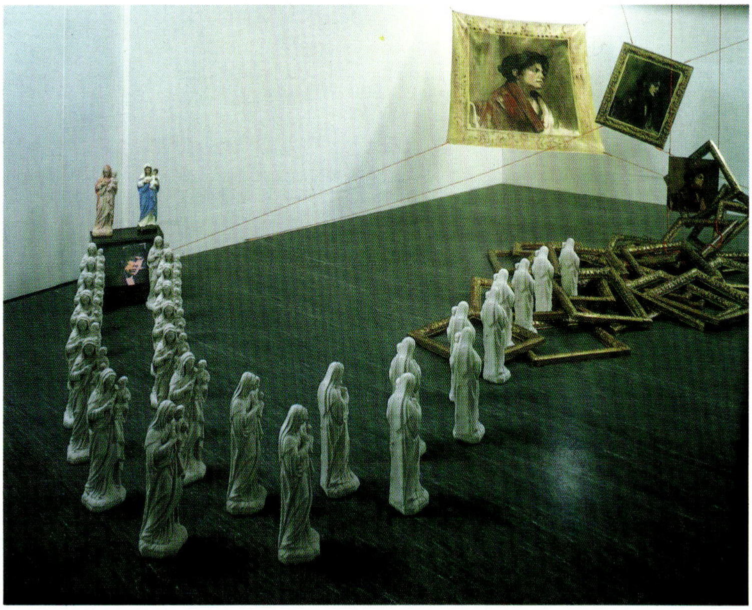

ARTIST'S NOTES My choice here was to emphasise the positive sides and not to exaggerate the level of the negative sides in organising this exhibition. This was not in order to curry favour with the other organisers or to pretend that this exhibition is any better than it is. It is because of the history of women and women's criticism of themselves in public and the effect that has on people who are not feminists. So, if I sit here going through all this bitchy arguing and fighting and jealousy and rivalry and competition all this that goes on in every group exhibition I have ever been in – then you would walk out of this room, thinking this is yet another women's show – you would not remember that this happens in all group exhibitions. You would label it yet again as a reinforcement of the stereotyping of women. That is why I am here determined to go on saying, that it's everyone's in this room, and everyone's, who has been to this exhibition, responsibility to make a future for women artists.

That means creating exhibitions – whatever the difficulties, whatever the costs and with whatever situations are possible – with whatever beliefs you have (once you are informed about the issues), if you hold them sincerely, if you have questioned them deeply, and if you believe in them. – and not to keep concentrating on the fact that in every single situation that mankind has undertaken (and that is supposed to include women), because we are not gods, has been imperfect. I don't believe that there is any 'right' way of doing any of what we are trying to do. I think that there are as many ways as there are women, – and that there are as many systems. And the trouble is that we have an overwhelmingly strong system based on male values. To begin to change that system, some women have had to move into that system and adopt some of its values in terms of the nature of the space we are now exhibiting in. At least here we have ideas based on the primacy of female values, understood and held in the works. The works may be showing within a building and within an organisation that has been unsympathetic, but nevertheless this is an achievement. To have small exhibitions where women have more contact, to have enormous exhibitions, where women have total control – fantastic. I hope, within my life-time we'll see all these things. I hope within my life-time we'll see women's work taken as seriously and judged as harshly as men's – but with a true understanding of women's values by the art world.

This is just one event, which has taken many women a lot of effort and a lot of time to organise. For myself, taking part in it has been another reassurance, that I am in the right place, that I am making art, doing an occupation that women for hundreds of years have done successfully. For me one of the greatest tragedies among women is, that we are all too hungry for change and so every achievement of every group of women meets criticism from other women because it is not perfect. Now this exhibition is a great achievement, it is a great step forward, it's not perfect – thank God. Women have been conditioned for far too long that we should be perfect, that we should be Madonnas. This is not a reality. We will make mistakes – constantly – that is our right as human beings, that is one sort of freedom!

Rose Garrard, 'Kunst mit Eigen-Sinn' conference, Vienna, 1985

SITES

I 'Rose Garrard' ICA London

II 'Kunst mit Eigen-Sinn' Museum of the 20th Century Vienna

III 'Dadarama' Riverside Studios London

IV 'Living Art' Guinness Hop Store Dublin

COMPONENTS

Multi-media installation with 30 plaster madonnas, 30 cast frames, 3 replicas of the 'Concours' oil painting, continuous play video with bird soundtrack.

Preparatory Drawing

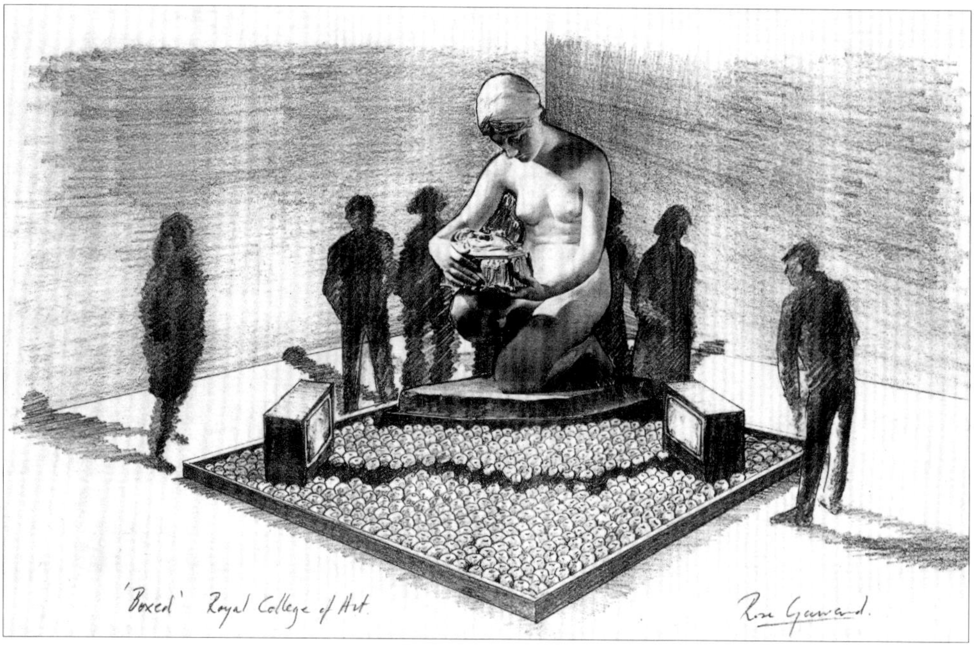

ARTIST'S NOTES I'm not interested in replacing a rigid system, based mainly on male values, but very much conspired by women in the support of male values, I'm not interested in replacing that rigid system with an equally rigid system brought about by people who call themselves feminists. And if anyone in this room believes that 'feminism' is a fixed dogma then they are not feminists in my eyes. For me feminism is a creative, progressive questioning, which is very much like the process that I believe art has always been. Though I consider myself a feminist, I do not make feminist art. I make art. Art has room for everybody, we do not have to put ourselves outside of art, outside of history. We have to make sure that history and art are changed by us to include us. And that our work, our thoughts and our values are held as equal to those of men and that they are as effective in how they are read.

Rose Garrard, 'Kunst mit Eigen-Sinn' conference, Vienna, 1985

SITE

'Cross Currents' Royal College of Art London

COMPONENTS

Approximately two hundred red apples, two video tapes and monitors, two photo silhouettes of Pandora by Harry Bates and 50 postcards.

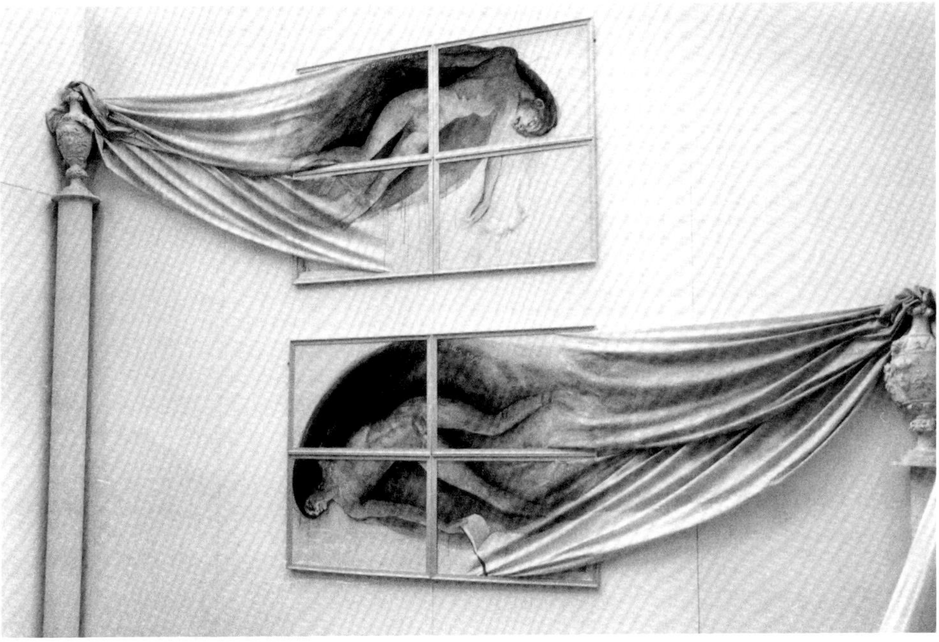

ART PRESS I have left the best till last. Rose Garrard and Helen Chadwick are both outstanding. They consider the role of women in today's society; without stridency; with sensitivity and sympathy ... Garrard's installation continues her pre-occupation with Pandora, this time comprising a tableau in pink and blue where Adam and Eve – or eternal man and woman – live out their lives between grief and guns; sweet joy and swallows.

Claire Henry, Studio International, Autumn 1984

ARTIST'S NOTES I won't give up looking at either a male or a female image. There is always a danger for women artists that they can't produce a female nude because the language for reading the female nude is so heavily weighted with male values. There is a danger that it is impossible within feminist theory, or has been until recently, to support the production of a female nude image by a woman artist, particularly one which is about sensuality or sexuality, because of the difficulty of it being read in any other but this male context.

So a lot of work has been done to change these traditional patriarchal contexts in which images appear and are read, and I suppose that's where I'm primarily working at the moment. I'm trying to clarify the prejudiced meanings that exist and trace them to their origins in history and myth. There's still a lot of work to be done, to establish feminist contexts for work which will allow a female language to develop.

Rose Garrard in conversation with Marion Roberts (of Birmingham Post) 1984

POPULAR PRESS People do not give up power voluntarily unless it is in their own self interest. Why should men change, just because women expect them to? They have the upper hand at every level – the personal, political, economic, sexual – and in the family.

The only way men will be persuaded to give up their supremacy will be if they themselves begin to value the aspects of life denied to them. This means believing that it is as damaging to deny gentleness to men as to deny ambition and aggression to women. It means valuing parenthood as much as we value banking. It means valuing the personal and the private lives of people as much as their working and public lives.

Polly Toynbee, The Guardian, January 1987

SITE

'Aperto' 41st Venice Biennale 1984

COMPONENTS

Four large scale paintings on calico with plaster objects, vases and columns.

Photograph
Steve Collins

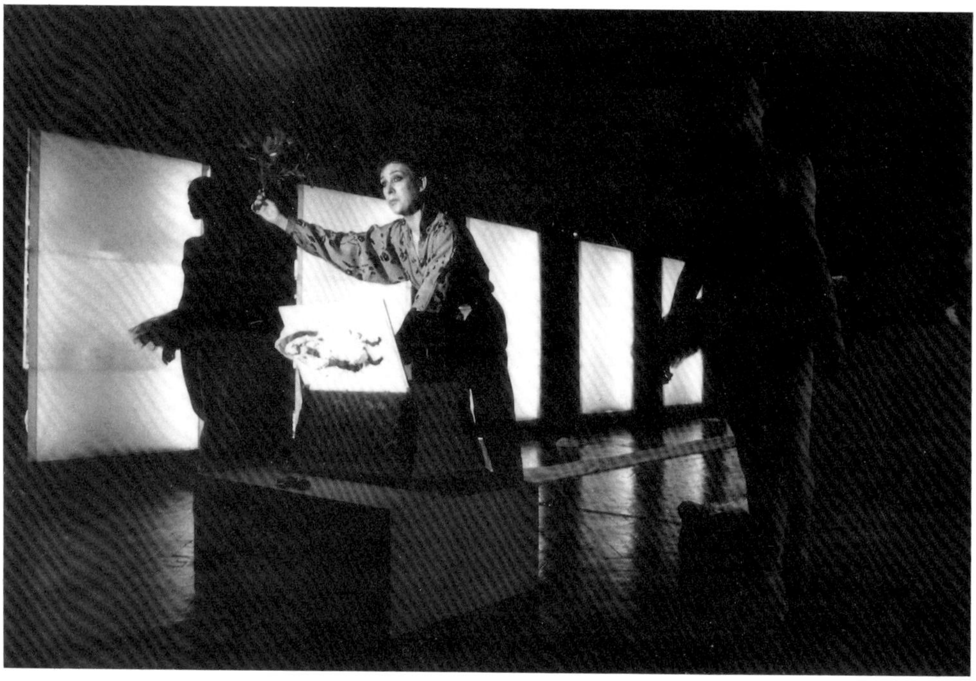

ARTIST'S NOTES Due to the restrictions of 'gigging' performances; the limited set up time, the short fixed duration and traditional separation between artist and audience, I hadn't worked in this way for some time. When I was invited to create this new short piece I decided to be quite mischievous,working with a variety of filmic and theatrical conventions, lighting, sound effects, costumes and characters, (Magician, Chaplin, Hitler, and Bride) so that I 'inhabited' the theatrical image, its pretence and trickery, but placed these roles like quotations within the real-time of the live event.

The increasingly influential weight of 'feminist theory' had, I felt, led to an outright condemnation of certain sexually stereotyped professions in which women had been able to be successful. I was interested in re-examining some of these, and having worked with the starlet images of Monroe and Garland, I now wanted to explore the role of the ballerina in more depth. Projects U.K. found two very young dancers whose confident, disciplined and powerful performances of this distortion of the feminine raised many previously unvoiced questions regarding the motivations for becoming such a 'model'.

Rose Garrard 1994

SITE

Laing Art Gallery Newcastle upon Tyne

COMPONENTS

Two young female ballet dancers and the artist as performers. Three interior lit boxes, books, guns, masks, madonnas, bunches of flowers. Audio sound track, script, and video. Bridal gown, Chaplin/Hitler costumes and ballet tutus

COMMISSION

Projects U.K. Newcastle upon Tyne organised by Jon Bewley.

Photograph
Ikon Gallery
Birmingham

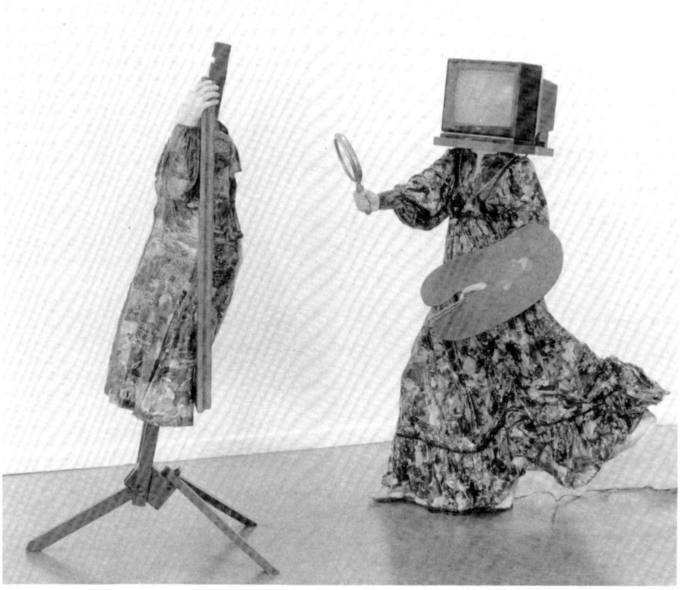

ART PRESS The two standing figures in the recent sculpture 'La Pittura', are clothed in tradition – the artist in a dress printed with Vermeer's paintings of women, the model clothed in a dress of sentimental nineteenth century images – yet the sculptures are leaping out of the conventions which confine the woman artist. For Garrard's voice issuing from the T.V. monitor head of the first figure over a video montage of 'lost' and anonymous women artists, invokes the transcendent union of opposites within, '... I am the utterance of my name. I am the whore and the holy one, do not banish me from your sight, and do not make your voice hate me, nor your hearing. I am knowledge and ignorance, I am strength and I am fear. I am the one whom you have scattered, and you have gathered me together. I am the knowledge of my inquiry, and the finding of those who seek after me. I am within ... I am the utterance of my name.'

The text she has adapted from 'The Thunder, Perfect Mind', a 2000 year old gnostic hymn, admits despair and exhilaration, pollution and purity to co-exist at once. Though this text relates to the exalted Sapiential of the Old Testament in which Hokma, the Wisdom of God, speaks in female voice, it refuses to anathematise in the Judaeo-Christian mode. The all-inclusiveness of its antithesis, and the forgivingness of its mysticism, make it a characteristic mirror of Rose Garrard's spirit; she has struggled against the sectarianism of some feminist artists, for an encompassing, humane tolerance of difference and an understanding of the Other. Although Garrard lifts off the layers which obscure the person lost in our forgettings, though she has reworked an ecstatic text giving voice to the pre-eminent feminine principle, she never adopts an essentialist position in her recovery of female actions and potential.

Marina Warner, 'Redressing the Balance' NGBK, Berlin 1987

ARTIST'S NOTES Video. Woman artist as her own model, forgotten names, forgotten faces, remembered through the image, through the self portrait. The artist turning to face herself throughout five hundred years ... the active model banished by mythology ... the subject of her own gaze. Woman as maker of art ... struggling not to clothe herself in the passive model ... disguarded by history, but being gathered together again.

'La Pittura The Spirit of Painting Reclaimed' was completed in December 1986, and the life size female figures of artist and model were constructed from two dresses bought in a second-hand clothing shop. The model's dress is made from fabric printed with romantic images of Victorian women in crinolins and parasoles walking in picturesque landscapes. However, the dress has a utilitarian cut for everyday maternity wear.The artist's dress is made from fabric printed with reproductions of Vermeer's paintings of working women models, but ironically this fabric is cut into a full length evening-dress with an empire line and frills at the hem.

Rose Garrard 1987

SITES

'Conceptual Clothing' Ikon Gallery Birmingham &
Harris Museum and Art Gallery Preston
Peterborough City Museum and Art Gallery
Spacex Gallery Exeter
Stoke on Trent City Museum and Art Gallery
Aberdeen Art Gallery
Huddersfield Art Gallery
Cartwright Hall Bradford

COMPONENTS

Two life size resin and fibreglass figures, one with video monitor head and continuous play video with soundtrack derived from gnostic texts.

Photograph
Yoko Terauchi

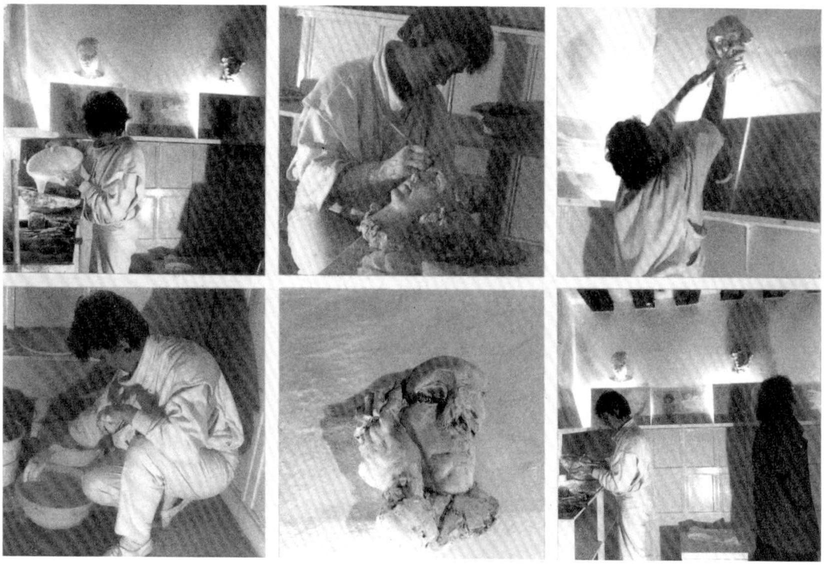

ARTIST'S NOTES The newspaper, open at page three, lay on the only unoccupied seat. She tried to ignore the image, but knew that its presence had already effected her own. Her moments hesitation had been noticed. Now they were anticipating a response.

Daily throughout September 1986 I bought The Sun newspaper and cast page three into plaster. Each day I also worked from self-portraits by women artists, modelling their faces and setting the empty moulds into the newspaper panels beside the 'topless' models. Through this private ritualised task I hoped to explore and question the restrictions effecting the apparent choice between woman as stereotyped model and woman as creative role model. Quotations expressed the inner experience of women artists whose practice has taken them beyond the limitations of the feminine gender stereotype. 'Casting Room One' was installed in a vacant newspaper shop in Canterbury as part of 'Third Generation : Women Sculptors', and I was present for six days of ritualised live work, casting up positive heads of women artists from the distorted clay pulled from the original moulds. During this public process the implications of the work, the roles of artist and model, the visual evidence of women artists becoming their own active models, the limitations and distortions experienced by women when trying to become culturally visible, and many of the present and future possibilities for change, were discussed with visitors. Through these ritualised tasks I was able to join with the public in questioning the systems and processes of distortion, which perpetuate the image of the stereotyped model while consigning creative role models for women to historical oblivion. Seeing both 'models' from inside out, a sense of the shared anonymity of women emerged and the price of the struggle to become 'visible' became the focus of the enquiry.

Rose Garrard 1986

ART PRESS The phrase 'actions to reveal the distortion process' recurs in the script which motivates the installation 'Casting Room One: An Historical Experiment', but it could also be applied to Garrard's oeuvre as a whole. She reveals, often poignantly, that the subject can never be fully realised, in memory or in art, that the paper on which the fingerprints are taken is always watermarked, as it were, with history, and that this history, in the case of women and their place in the visual arts obliterates their names and their work both as models and artists, and denies them individual character. By holding up that watermark to the light, Garrard uncovers from forgetfulness, the lives and work of female artists both living and dead.

It is a rite of commemoration, unobtrusive and effective. In the publication of the calendar girl poses and the impersonal inventory of taped information, a restrained irony jolts the voyeur into awareness of the pin-ups' historically muted, colonised condition, and makes their anonymity visible. With the concave moulds of the artists' self-portrait displayed in negative, and distorted positive casts hung above, Garrard reaffirms that all history is a distortion, that the artists "attempted to represent themselves, yet above all, I'm owning up to the fact that in the act of replicating I cannot avoid distorting yet again."

Marina Warner, 'Redressing the Balance', NGBK, Berlin 1987

SITE

Empty Shop Unit 'Third Generation: Women Sculptors' Canterbury Festival

COMPONENTS

Twelve sculpted portrait heads of women artists, from past and present. Twenty one plaster panels incorporating page three of The Sun, hollow moulds and quoted texts from women artists, audio tape, three shelves, neon back lighting, and artist as performer in white clothing

COMMISSION

Drew Gallery 'Third Generation: Women Sculptors' Canterbury Festival.

Photograph
Phillip Brice

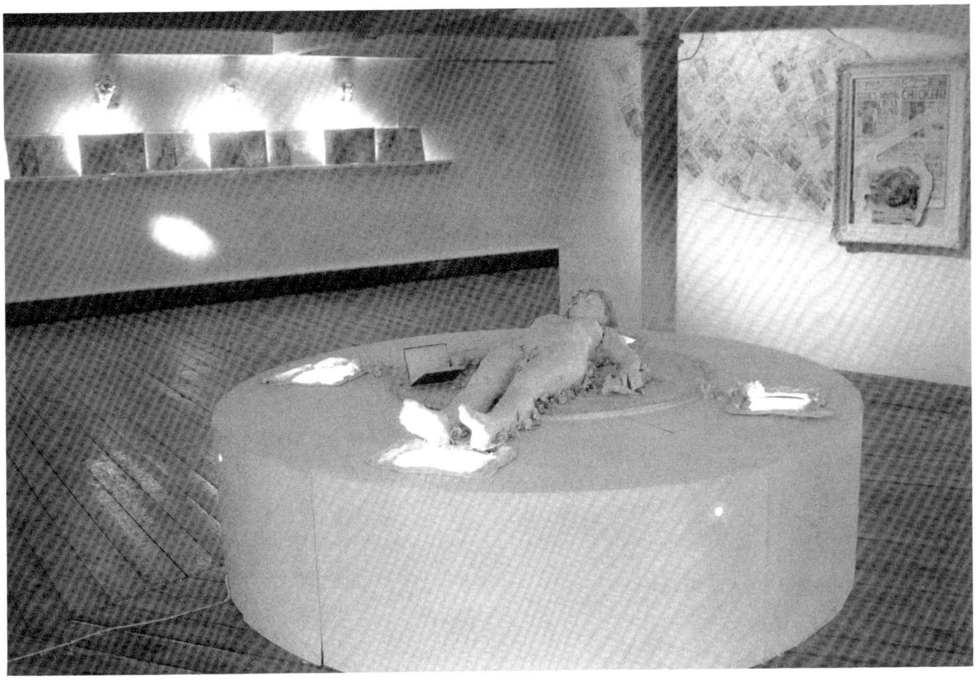

Shelf No. 6

I can't live where I want to. I can't go where I want to. I can't even say what I want to. I decided I was very stupid not at least to paint as I wanted to.

Georgia O'Keeffe

Shelf No.14

I didn't stand naked in front of three hundred people because I wanted to be fucked, but because my sex and work were harmoniously experienced I could have the audacity or courage to show the body as a source of varying emotive power.

Carolee Schneeman

Shelf No. 18

Yes, it is my work that comes between us, but I cannot put that out of my life because it is too much of myself now. If I had not my love for painting I should be a different person. I am really certain that I could never live with you sexually day after day ... at any rate I am sure I could not work at all if I lived with you every day.

Dora Carrington

Shelf No.20

The spirit of art is always affirming, even when it deals with painful realities, for the act of making an image transforms that pain into something beautiful. This act has been what has sustained me, no matter how hard life has been.

Judy Chicago

Photograph
Phillip Brice

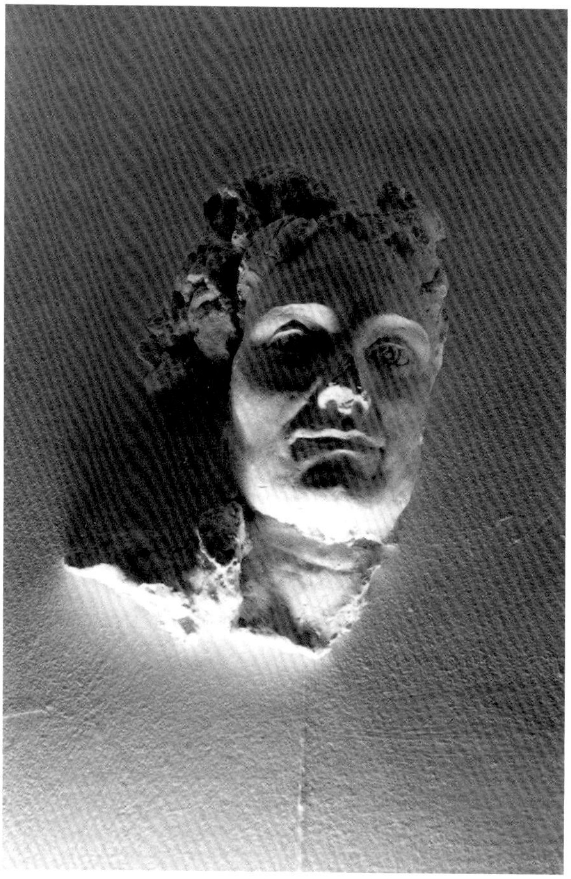

ARTIST'S NOTES 'Violent Incident : 1935 – 1962 – 1986', a wood and plaster panel, was the first 'unit' in this work in which I attempted to deal directly with issues raised by the images of women sensationalised by the popular press. It is to me a work which not only commemorates the death of Norma Jeane Baker but the many thousands of women who have died and will continue to die violently in a culture which distorts and fears the expression of female sexuality, and ridicules the pacifist beliefs and values of women.

Monroe not only persistently claimed to have been raped as a child (1935) but recent published research alleges that tapes made by Bernard Spindel placed Robert Kennedy 'with her when she died' on the night when 'some sort of violent incident' was recorded (August 4 1962). The entire contents of these tapes confiscated by the District Attorney's investigators in 1966, and most of the FBI files on Monroe compiled for J. Edgar Hoover which designated her a potential risk to national security, remain to this day a closely guarded secret. A few heavily censored reports reveal that in the weeks immediately preceding her death she discussed 'significant questions' including 'the morality of atomic testing' with friends who were thought to have left wing and Mafia connections. At that time she also allegedly had a blinding row with Robert Kennedy over Cuba, one that led him to tell her she was 'turning communist'. She was scheduled to hold a press conference concerning these issues but died just before this was possible. On a US Television News interview in 1985 Marilyn's autopsy surgeon was asked if her death had been a murder. He looked straight into the camera, nodded, and said 'Could be.'

The juxtaposition of today's newspaper headlines with the famous photos of Monroe with her dress blowing up (May 16 1986, 'Stars Mum Raped' The Sun, 'Chicken! Fears over Libya' The Star) seems highly insensitive to the violence of Norma Jeane Baker's life and death. Also when related to women's present 'Fears' of world violence and personal 'Rape', the underlying double standards become increasingly offensive. They contain a particularly cruel irony for me. Tomorrow I have arranged a video shoot at my Hackney Wick studio of an actress wearing a replica of Marilyn's white dress ... a location which coincidentally overlooks the spot on the river Lea where earlier this year the raped and strangled body of a young woman was discovered. This violent incident, always in my mind when I work there after dark, also remains unsolved.

Rose Garrard, May 16 1986

Photograph
Phillip Brice

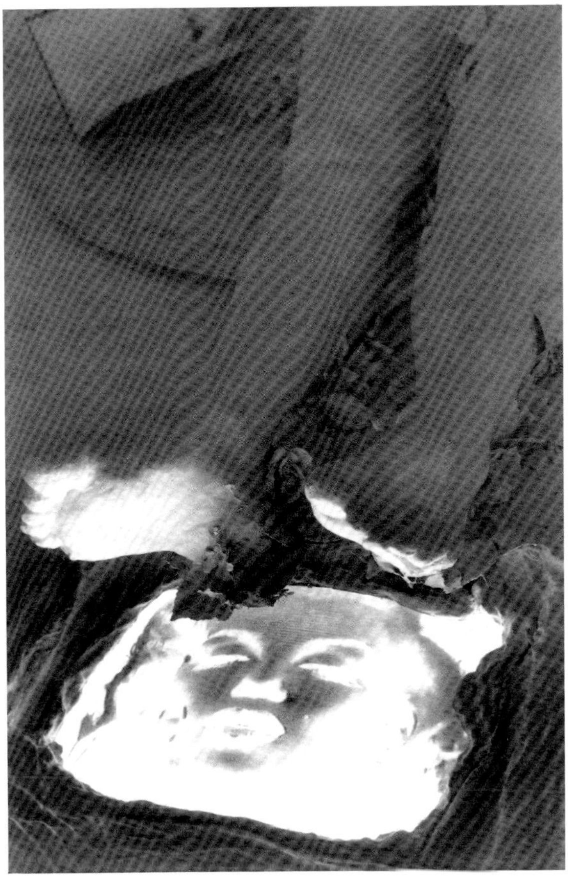

ART PRESS In this piece, Garrard's fidelity to whiteness as a metaphor for women's invisibility gains mordancy, for Monroe alive could not have achieved the necessary status of the idol who must be immune to time. Without death, Monroe, who would be 61 today, could not occupy the sacred site of the eternal, the necessary state of the object of worship. Within the installation, through the plaster panel 'Violent Incident: 1935 - 1962 - 1986' Garrard also acknowledges the necrophilia present in the cult of the female idol through the alleged rape and mysterious death of Monroe, connecting the violence against women and against humanity pervasive in contemporary life by reproducing front pages of newspapers where Monroe's image appears next to headlines of rape and the bombing of Libya. The photograph from 'Some Like it Hot' appears in the newspapers to illustrate the report of the theft of the same white pleated dress from an exhibition. 'Casting Room Two' questions the relation between male desire and female identity, with the meditative sympathy typical of Rose Garrard's work. Again, as in the earlier Pandora pieces, the history book Norma Jeane holds is blank, and the dove in the other hand of the supine figure appears as the symbol of hope which the first woman released from the jar. In the continuing circle of time, there is a future as well as a past. Yet encircled by the words 'The Bride stripped bare by her bachelors even again and again...' Norma Jeane also occupies the present.

But the prettiness of the ornament covering Norma Jeane's effigy is deliberate: Garrard is committed to retrieving traditional female skills and pleasures from disdain. Here the 'decorative' flowers which mask the nakedness of Norma Jeane's face and genitals are those traditional tokens of love; the rose, whose ancient meaning was as a recognised symbol for the positive beauty of the female vulva. Garrard aligns herself with feminists like Roszika Parker who have argued convincingly that the pejorative value accorded to adornment and other female pursuits by the patriarchy should not mean they are to be rejected by women themselves. It is striking that the greater distance an artistic activity places itself from the experience of the senses, the more highly it ranks in this canon. In the patriarchal scheme; sewing, flower arranging, cookery, pottery, which entail direct manipulation, become 'minor' arts. But Garrard's sound track affirms 'Do not despise it because it is small and it is little, and do not turn away greatness in some parts from the smallnesses, for the smallnesses are known from the greatnesses.'

The identification of woman with nature, and her dilemma that she enters culture as a man-made object, clothed in male expectations, fears and desires, obviously lies at the foundation of Garrard's questioning.

Marina Warner, 'Redressing the Balance', NGBK, Berlin 1987

SITES

'Confrontations' Cornerhouse Manchester

'Redressing the Balance' NGBK Berlin Germany

'Shoemaker's Daughter' Air Gallery London

COMPONENTS

Life size sculpted fibreglass and resin figure of Norma Jeane Baker, framed plaster panel 'Violent Incident', four horizontal monitors in a circle with continuous play video and sound, incorporating 'Casting Room One: An Historical Experiment'

COMMISSION

Cornerhouse Manchester for 'Confrontations; The Role of Controversy in Art' organised by Rob la Frenais and Projects UK, Newcastle upon Tyne.

Photograph
Martin Coulton

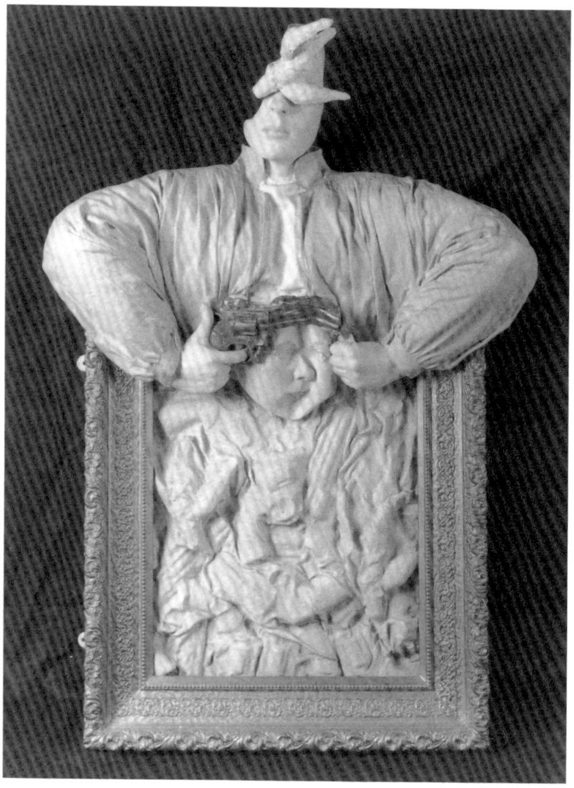

ART PRESS Many contemporary artists in Britain – Helen Chadwick, Susan Hiller, Mary Kelly – have now, like Rose Garrard become their own subjects and models in photographic and mixed media pieces which testify to their fantasies, feelings and memories. Garrard has frequently made replicas of herself in the past and of objects of talismanic importance to her, and her early work may have influenced the younger sculptor, Antony Gormley, who casts his own body in lead, but here in heiratic poses as perturbing totems of everyman.
Marina Warner, 'Redressing the Balance', NGBK, Berlin 1987

Rose Garrard has played with two and three dimensions to form one of the most exciting and enigmatic images of the show. She retains parts of a gilt picture frame, but out of the top section looms a fractured, hollow head with a bird in flight obscuring the face. Elbows and forearms clad in fibreglass folds of a real dress lead to hands holding a squashed infantile mask and a hand gun. Lower down, the innocent folds of the dress reveal more gun shapes. There are disturbing suggestions of birth, childhood, suicide, resurrection and the spirit.
Adrian Whittlesea, Artsite Gallery, Bath, September 1987

POPULAR PRESS The show is also significant in the large contribution by women artists, who constitute eleven out of the sixty one. Artists like Eileen Cooper, Mary Mabbut and Rose Garrard are well versed in self-portraiture. For years they have been using their own image to generalise about women in society. Rose Garrard's piece for instance, has a thinly veiled reference to child-birth.
The Independent, September 15 1987

ARTIST'S NOTES Though a self-portrait, this piece again uses the bird and gun as symbols of peace and violence, hope and anger, and through these represents the inner tensions and turmoils behind the public face of many women professionals, particularly artists, including myself.
'I cannot be something for everyone ... woman, beautiful, artist, wife, cook, saleslady, all these things. I cannot even be myself or know what I am' (Eva Hesse). There is no intentional reference to child-birth here, and certainly for me this isn't uppermost in the image. But some male writers seeing squirming forms in a female abdomen have drawn this conclusion, but quite what they make these guns mean in their context I don't know.
Rose Garrard 1987

SITES
'Self-Portrait: A Modern View' Artsite Gallery Bath and nationwide exhibition tour

COMPONENTS
Resin, fibreglass and mixed media relief incorporating gilt frame

COLLECTION
Nicholas Treadwell London.

Polo Ground in Wartime: The Four Horsemen … **1987**

Photograph
Nicola Percy

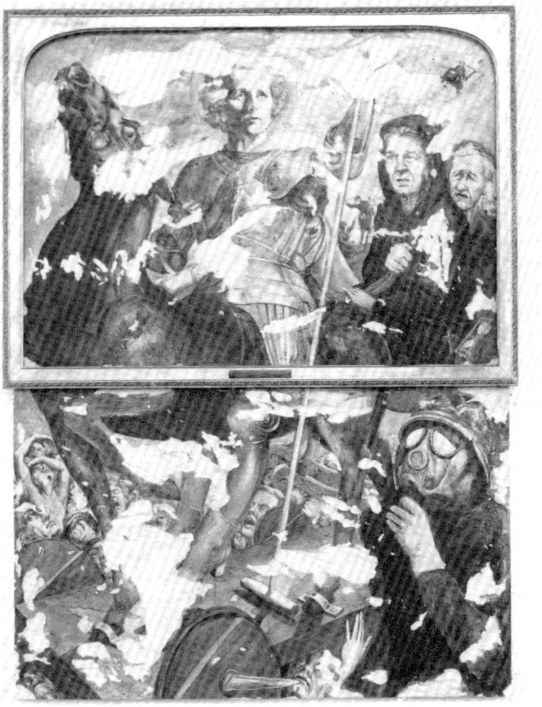

SITES

'Redressing the Balance' NGBK Berlin Germany

'Heroes' Air Gallery London

Drumcroon Wigan Education Art Centre

COMPONENTS

Acrylic painted plaster panel and gilt frame.

Beirut Blind: Re-cover Haji Acmhed Ali **1987**

Photograph
Dee Berridge

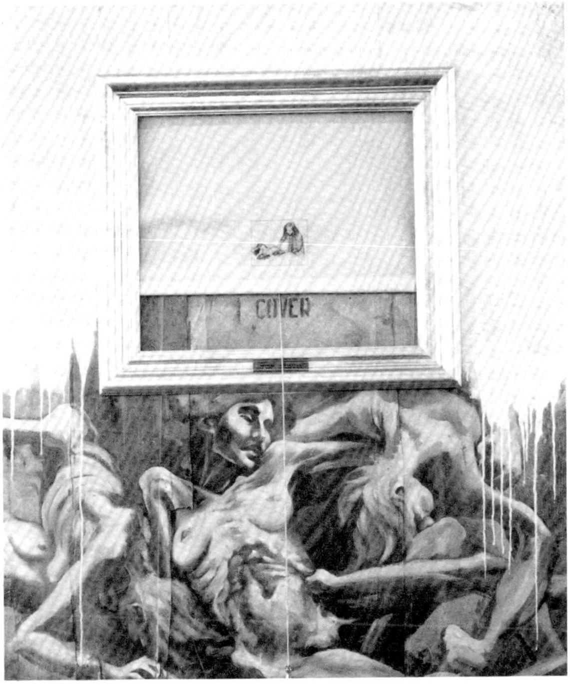

SITE

'Redressing the Balance' NGBK Berlin Germany

COMPONENTS

Oil paint and mixed media objects on wooden panel.

MATRIARCHY: BEATEN BY FEMININE POWER; 1950S PARTY DRESS. PORTRAIT, ELIZABETH VIGÉE-LE BRUN

Photograph
Nicola Percy

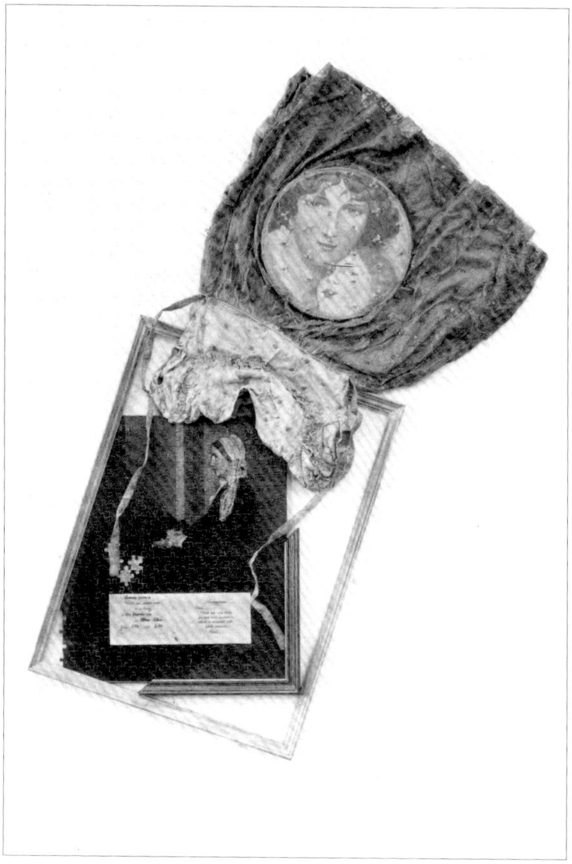

ART PRESS In 'Redressing the Balance' the installation seen for the first time in Berlin, Rose Garrard integrates many pieces of the puzzle she has addressed over twenty years of work, as she makes visible the culture with which she herself has been clothed, by means of the attire which she wore at different crucial stations in her life: her first party dress embroidered with roses, the overalls she used as an art student, the waitresses dress and apron of her first holiday job, the wedding suit she made herself. Her journey into memory achieves objective reality through these authentic relics, kept by her mother in the house near Worcester where she grew up, and she has incorporated them for real into the piece, so that they become its fabric, emblazoning the roles in which she, Rose Garrard, was herself cast. For the spectator, the experience as the piece unfolds becomes even more intimate because she has rubbed raw pigment into the resin, rather than covering anything over with paint, and in each case, an embroidery hoop encloses an untouched section of fabric on which is painted the portrait of a woman artist. Chosen for its connection to women's work and its symbolic roundness, this frame opens a window on to her past, like the monstrance which displays the presence of the relic. Rose Garrard never lapses into piety, but the formulae of the Catholic liturgy have influenced her; alongside each discarded garment the image of a female artist who inspired Garrard appears, like a votive image in a shrine: Louise Nevelson, Carolee Schneeman, Yoko Ono, have joined the pantheon of her earlier works.

Each section of 'Redressing the Balance' represents a phase through which Rose Garrard passed in her adaption to the order of female identity; they are also toilettes (toile, cloth or canvas; tekne, work, technical), outfits women put on to turn their face to the world ... when she narrates her own story in terms of the clothing she wore, she acknowledges the kinship between the concept of the image and the notions of woman, how both femininity and art are fabricated, worked, just as the cloth on which a picture is painted is itself worked or woven, and recognising this condition, she alerts us to its future possibilities with rare intelligence and sympathy, as well as unique imaginative power.

Marina Warner, 'Redressing the Balance', NGBK, Berlin, 1987

LITERACY: LINED UP IN A MAN'S WORLD; 1960S SCHOOL UNIFORM. PORTRAIT, BERTHE MORISOT

Photograph
Nicola Percy

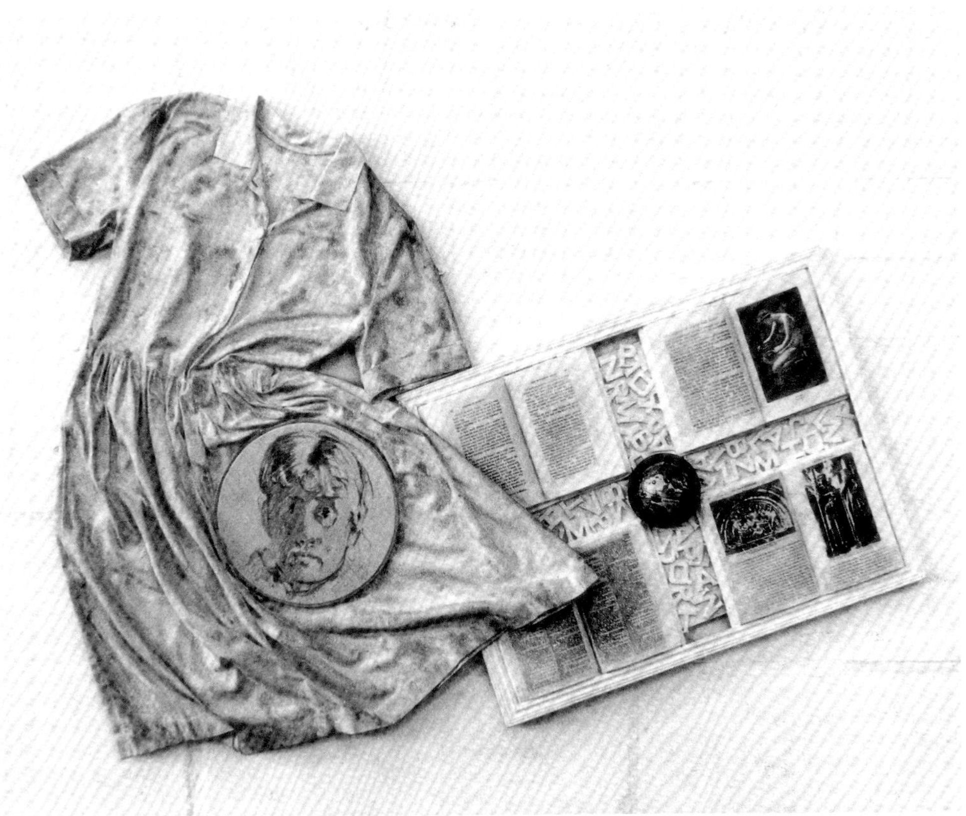

ARTIST'S NOTES Work on this installation began during the final stages of my divorce this year, and this experience as well as other personal factors; reaching the age of forty, my mother becoming suddenly 'old', are perhaps what led me to look again at my past. As my mother is becoming increasingly frail we are having to face her eventual move from her home and the reduction of her possessions. She constantly tries to give me things rather than face throwing them away or selling them. In her airing cupboard I found piles of neatly laundered clothes and discovered items of my own clothing, worn at different ages and for different roles ... my first party dress aged four, ballet tutu, waitress uniform, dance dress, wedding suit, etc, which now I couldn't bring myself to throw away. In the studio, I began using the clothes as stepping stones to retrace my own history. My mother has been pointing out objects, (postcards, books, magazines and pictures) which had always been at home but which I hadn't then known were of work by women artists. I want to re-examine my long held belief in the absence of women artists from my formative years and 'redress the balance'. Through the frames with the clothes I also want to identify the periods and systems by which I've been gender-conditioned; how I'd learnt not to see or expect a history of women as artists. Remembering times when I wore these clothes, I began to connect personal and world events (British H Bomb Tests, the deaths of Churchill, Monroe, and the assassination of J.F.Kennedy, the turning away of Cambodian boat people to drown, the death of Rudolf Hess, etc). Using embroidery frames as circular 'stretchers', I've begun painting relevant self portraits by 'absent' women artists, onto the clothing and coating the surrounding cloth with resin and pigments. The retracing of my past through these shed 'skins' (the clothes) has become a process of positive rediscovery, each a re-examination of my own process of becoming a woman and an artist.
Rose Garrard 1987

POPULAR PRESS Rose Garrard's 'Redressing the Balance' is a group of wall-mounted assemblages evoking the memory of women artists past and present. Each is Garrard's attempt to establish their identity with the painted image and collected objects. Consistent to them all is an article of clothing and a painted portrait, though in the case of Jan Haworth, an artist prominent in the sixties, persistent research has failed to uncover an image of her. Women disappear from even the most recent history, an example giving added significance to Garrard's rediscovery. Her quest is very much a personal one, but the pragmatic use of materials makes it to a public one. They prompt the viewer to research for themselves.
MC, City Limits, November 27 1988

Work in Progress

Photograph
Dee Berridge

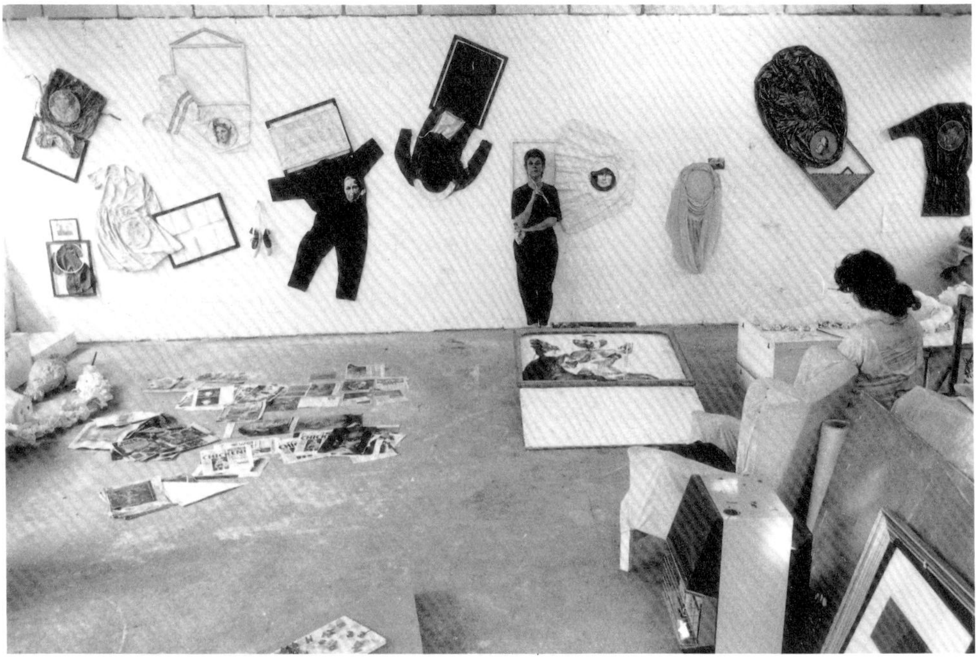

PATRIARCHY learning war games; 1940's Tom Boy Outfit
Portrait Artist, War Artist
MATRIARCHY beaten by feminine power; 1950's Party Dress
Portrait Artist, Elizabeth Vigée-Le Brun
ORTHODOXY dancing as they bomb Bikini Atoll; 1950's Tutu
Portrait Artist, Dame Laura Knight
LITERACY lined up in a man's world; 1960's School Uniform
Portrait Artist, Berthe Morisot
CULTURE absent from academia; 1960's Dance Dress
Portrait Artist, Angelica Kauffmann
DOMESTICITY waitressing at the banquet of life; 1960's Waitress Uniform Portrait Artist, Jan Howarth
SEXUALITY performing a dream morphology; 1960's Night Dress
Portrait Artist, Carolee Schneeman
MATRIMONY giving peace a chance; 1960's Wedding Suit
Portrait Artist, Yoko Ono
EDUCATION working within the system; 1970's Paris Overall
Portrait Artist, Louise Nevelson
ECONOMICS sinking in Venice while boat people drown; 1980's Biennale Dress. Portrait Artist, Artemisia Gentileschi
POLITICS eating the bread of life; 1980's Dinner Dress
Portrait Artist, Rose Garrard
HISTORY celebrating 750 years?; 1980's Berlin Dress
Portrait Artist, Kathe Kollwitz

SITES

'Redressing the Balance' NGBK Berlin Germany

Louise Hallett Gallery London

Drumcroon Wigan Education Art Centre

COMPONENTS

Twelve pieces of clothing from artist's childhood to 1987, on wood, resin and mixed media relief panels, with frames incorporating 'found' objects.

Photograph
Peter Silverleaf

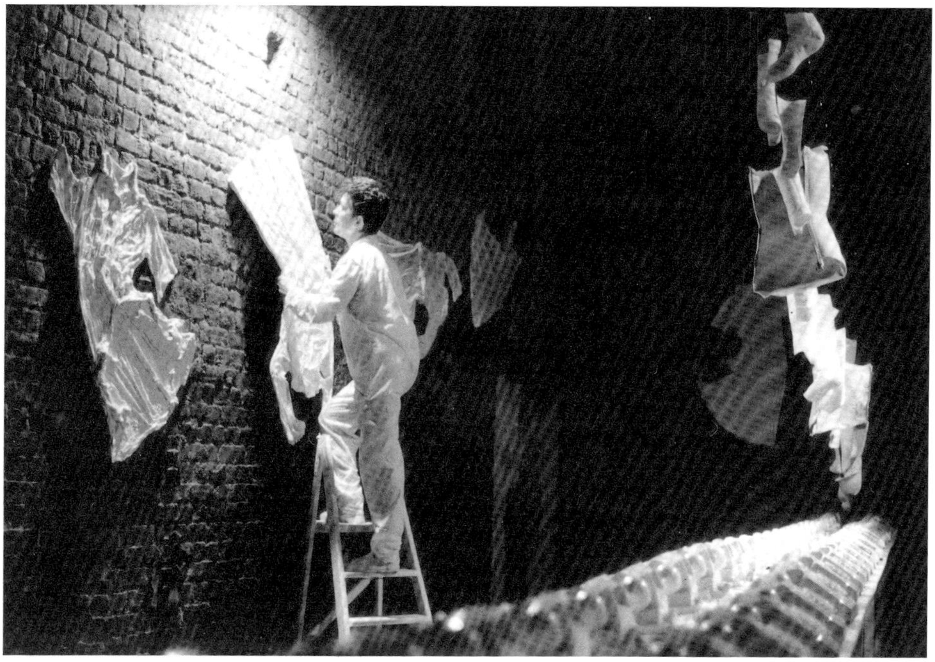

POPULAR PRESS As always, a significant personal event provided the catalyst for the 'Out of Line' piece. In this case it was a serious road accident earlier this year which put Garrard in the fractures ward of St Bartholomew's Hospital. She began recording the roles and behaviour of male and female patients, while her frequent visits for outpatient treatment brought her into contact with the adjoining meat market. 'Originally I saw strange analogies between the porters in the meatmarket carrying around lumps of death to give life, and the nurses in the hospital who try to cope with hunks of meat and bring them back to life.' The result was a complex work which extends from the cast from Garrard's arm to videos of television news footage of disasters. 'We're all so surprised when we have an accident, yet by recording ten days of news broadcasts you realise how we've created a world that relentlessly creates accidents.'

The shifting relationship between the sexes in Bart's was of special interest to her. Taped conversations with staff and patients provide the muttered cacophony in the Slaughterhouse that becomes clearly audible once the telephones receivers are picked up. The macho Irish builder, crippled by a falling load of bricks; the elderly man embarrassed by female nakedness in a mixed ward; the male nurse; the lonely old woman; all are treated with affection. Garrard prefers to analyse rather than moralise, but she does laugh at the recent memory of a male Polish artist, who, on visiting the Slaughterhouse and watching her installing the work, declared; 'Oh, so you're being a nurse!'.

'It immediately brought it all back,' she groans, 'the way that just being a woman and occupying women's roles is actually seen by other as a diminishment. First of all', she continues, 'the battle is to see yourself not as a diminishment and then to attempt actions that determine that in other people's eyes.'

Louisa Buck, The Guardian, November 3 1988

POPULAR PRESS Visitors can pick up a telephone and listen to the former owners of the plaster casts reminiscing about their ailments. According to the festival organisers, the exhibition 'explores the relationships between mind and body, inner and outer, male and female, during the process of physical healing'. But Mr David Hyams, leader of the council's Social Democratic opposition, said: 'It's the daftest arts display since the pile of bricks at the Tate. They're taking the mickey at the ratepayers' expense'.

Evening Standard, September 15 1988

Photograph
Jez Coulson

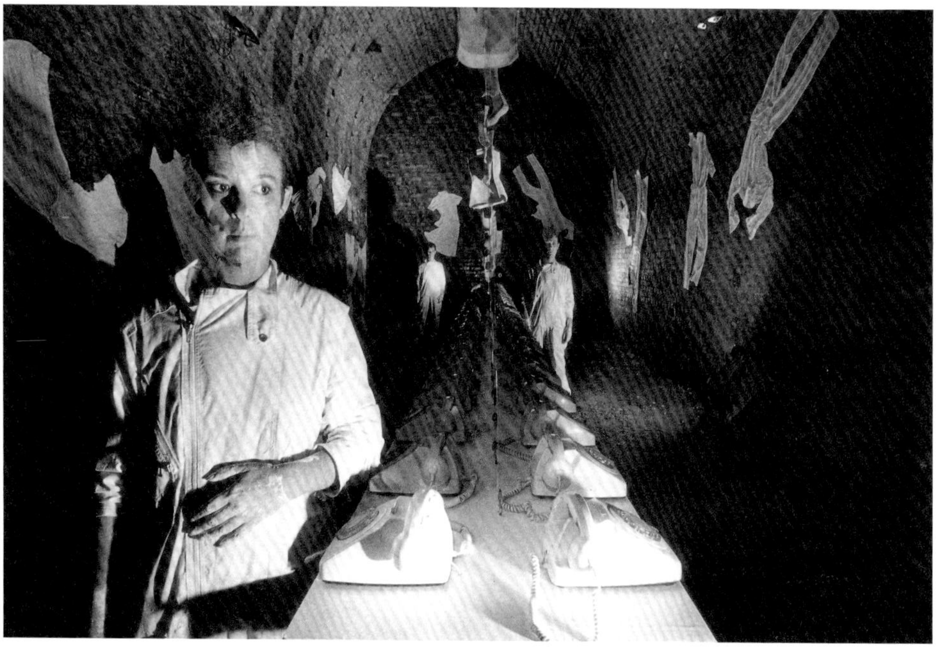

ART PRESS Over in a damp, malign slaughterhouse adjacent to London's meat market, Garrard's installation and live work drew from the artist's experiences while at a hospital following an accident. Observing the differing roles and behaviour of the male and female staff and patients at St Bartholomew's. Garrard produced a work that surveyed the gestalt of the healing process: clothes are as plaster casts, banks of phones a bureaucratic backbone, and the bewildering hospital administration and its power and gender organisation portrayed through the metaphor.
Oliver Bennet, New Art Examiner, February 1989

ARTIST'S NOTES On the 12 January I met with Rob la Frenais to decide the site for my forthcoming Edge 88 piece. I selected the Slaughterhouse site, originally an underground cold store for meat, on the north side of Smithfield Market. Two weeks later I was seriously injured in a motorbike accident outside Liverpool Street Station and was taken to St Bartholomew's Hospital, ironically, also beside the meat market.
Because of my concussion I only have vague memories of the days after this, but about a week later I do remember the dull thud of realisation that as the sites were in such close proximity the two contexts presented an amazing possibility for a new work. I also remember making a series of sketches of the other patients in my part of the ward, remarkably noisy elderly women, many of whom were dying. Most of the patients in the adjacent male section were young motorbike casualties who were mobile enough to constantly monopolise the only portable telephone. Nearly all of the women, including myself, were bedridden and unable to retrieve the phone ourselves. This caused considerable distress amongst the women, and I became increasingly anxious that I couldn't easily contact the outside world. The organisers of my three impending solo exhibitions didn't yet know that I was injured and would have to postpone some of the shows to later in the year.
I wasn't really aware of the extent of my injuries and rather stupidly ignored the surgeon's advice, signing myself out of hospital after ten days in order to get access to a telephone. As soon as I was home I contacted everyone and put back all the exhibitions I could, making Edge 88 the first in a closely packed showing schedule starting from September. In order for the bones in my shoulder and ribs to realign themselves I had to keep gently moving and so I began some large drawings based on simple washes, which became the 'Talisman' series. It was only now that I began to realise how serious my injuries were. I couldn't dress, wash, or prepare food for myself, lie, stand or sit in one position for long and I was afraid of going out at all in case anyone brushed against my broken bones, which apart from my left arm, were unprotected. I am tremendously indebted to a small group of supportive friends who helped me throughout this period, aiding my recovery, but at the time this unaccustomed degree of dependence on others, coupled with the strangeness of these new physical limitations, were very frustrating.
Rose Garrard 1994

Photograph
Peter Silverleaf

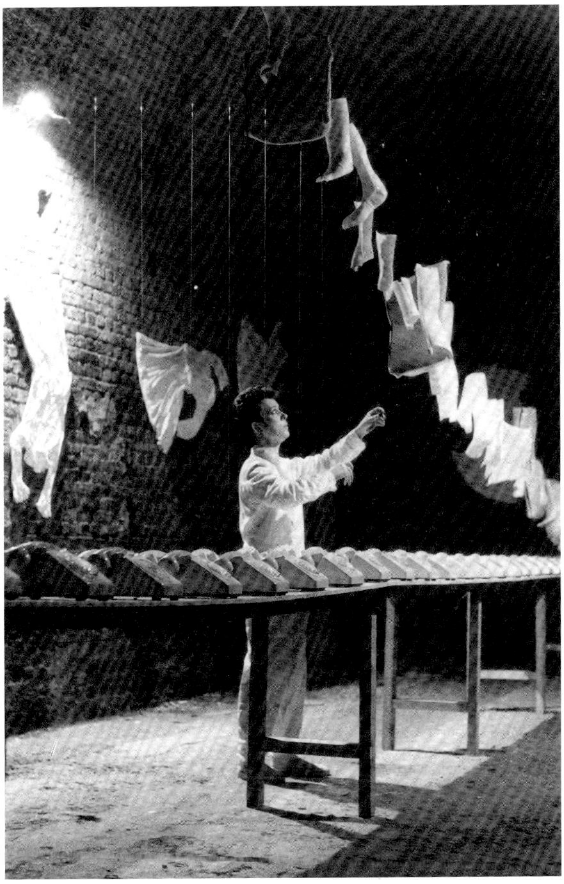

ARTIST'S NOTES Each time my arm cast was replaced I discussed the techniques and materials used and soon the cast-maker and I were debating the distinctions drawn between his professional activities and those of a sculptor. I told him about my ideas for Edge 88 and he began saving me examples of his 'best work' for inclusion in the show.

As part of my physiotherapy I was given ultra-sound treatment, and when I asked how this worked the therapist explained that severe physical shock alters the natural polarity of body cells but they change back towards normal with these particular sound frequencies. We speculated on the effects that music might be having on the body, and later this led me to wire up the body casts to pick-up heads, connecting them to amplifiers in the exhibition, to see what notes emerged when they were touched, and how visitors would respond.

I met with Rob again in early March at the site to finalise the plans of the new live work and installation. Following each of my twice weekly physiotherapy sessions I began making taped interviews with staff and patients at the hospital, asking them about their worries whilst in hospital and what basic things would help relieve their anxieties. Easy access to a telephone and to their own clothing emerged as the two main elements which patients felt would put them most at ease, reducing the stress they were under and so making them feel better. Eventually these edited audio tapes were played through the handsets of fifty telephones which could be lifted and listened to by visitors.

Throughout the first five days of the exhibition I worked live, carrying out a series of tasks including carrying buckets of water, stirring plaster, lifting plaster dipped clothes, smoothing them, carrying and hanging them up, all based on actions I needed to undertake to strengthen my arm and shoulder as part of my physiotherapy. These private motivations behind my public activity were not known by visitors at the time.

Rose Garrard 1993

SITES

'Edge 88' Biennale of Experimental Art
Slaughterhouse Smithfield London

'New Work Newcastle' Charlotte Square Newcastle upon Tyne

COMPONENTS

Ten tape recorders (sponsored by Rumbelows). Fifty telephones (sponsored by British Telecom) placed on a 32ft table. Casting/operating table and light. Emergency blue flashing light, selected hospital limb and torso casts. Recorded conversations with patients and staff at St Bartholomew's Hospital. Video monitor showing accidents reported on TV news. Quantity of men's and women's folded white clothing, plaster of paris, white mixing buckets and a white ladder. Artist as performer for five days in white clothing

COMMISSION

Edge 88 Biennale of Experimental Art.

The Wooden Box from her Father

Photograph
Louise Hallett Gallery

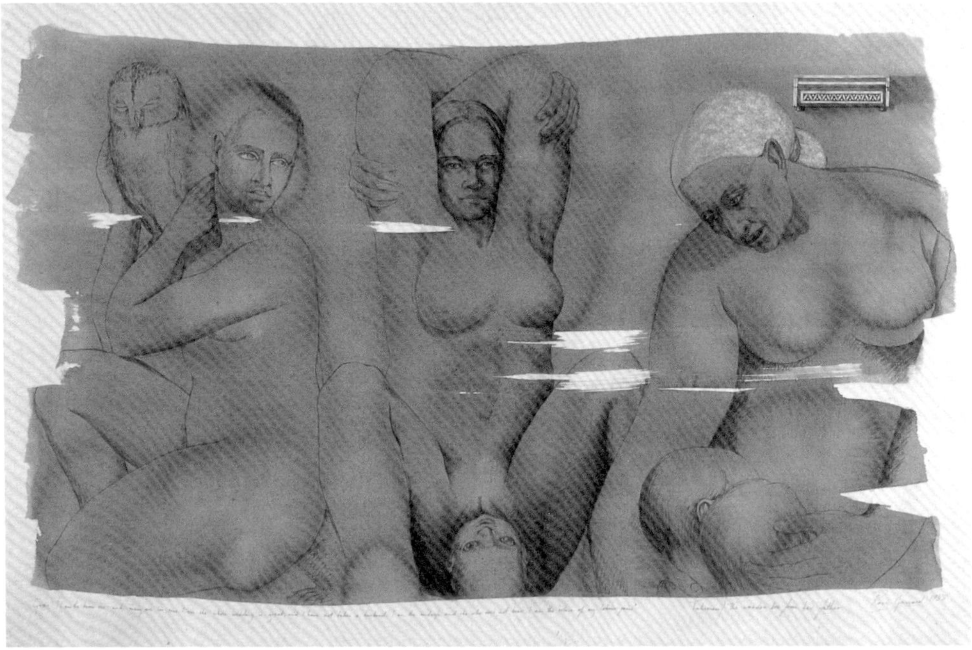

ART PRESS The inspiration behind this series of mixed media drawings, entitled 'Talisman', is taken from the two thousand year old gnostic text, 'The Thunder, Perfect Mind', which was re-discovered in 1946. This work is a continuation of the artist's quest for the reclamation of the past, both as woman and artist.

The twelve drawings in 'Talisman' were created during the artist's convalescence after an accident, and are based upon this gnostic text which was given to Rose Garrard by a friend, and which she found particularly strengthening during that period of healing. The painting process was a gnostic one, with the artist responding purely to the mental images that appeared when meditating on the wash she had put on the paper.

The text, which is spoken by a female voice in the first person, is that of the feminine principle within the spiritual Godhead. The work appeals to the feminine within us all, whether male or female; it is an appeal; it acknowledges the duality of the sexes, yet creatively recognises the fusion of opposites.

Jane Epstein 'Talisman', Louise Hallett Gallery, London 1988

Her hospitalisation and consequent convalescence physically prevented her from making the sort of work she had been doing prior to the accident but it also gave her the time to 're-examine why my art had been what it was, and see how it could become something different.' The 'something different' came about partly as a result of her injuries. Confined to bed with numerous broken bones she would apply transparent washes of paint to large sheets of paper and then 'stare at them for hours and hours and these groups of figures appeared just straight from the wash.' In drawing up the images which appeared from the accidental patterns of the wash she realised that the drawings related directly to a gnostic text she had been working with, seeming to illustrate passages from it.

The Oxford Dictionary defines gnostic as 'early Christian heretics claiming knowledge of spiritual mysteries', but Rose's specific interest in them lies in their concern with the feminine God. She claims that when the male disciples formulated the bible all the female texts were literally buried. The discovery of these texts has shed new light on the history of women and given Rose the opportunity to reclaim the distant past. The resulting series of drawings, collectively entitled 'Talisman' each bear a line of the text and Rose has superimposed a trompe l'oeil painting of an object from her childhood on to the group of figures. She feels that the 'Talisman' drawings are a new departure for her and one which she is looking forward to developing. They explore another layer of women's conditioning, one which extends back almost to the dawn of history, and which surviving evidence can only hint at.

What is clear is that Rose Garrard's talent lies in her ability to deal with these issues, issues of universal importance, in such a way as to make them relevant to each of us as an individual. By reclaiming her past she provides us with a mirror in which we can examine our own conditioning and ask questions about our identity.

Bryan Edmondson 'Portrait of the Artist as a Woman' Drumcroon, Wigan Education Art Centre 1991

The Leather Glove of her Mother

Photograph
Louise Hallett Gallery

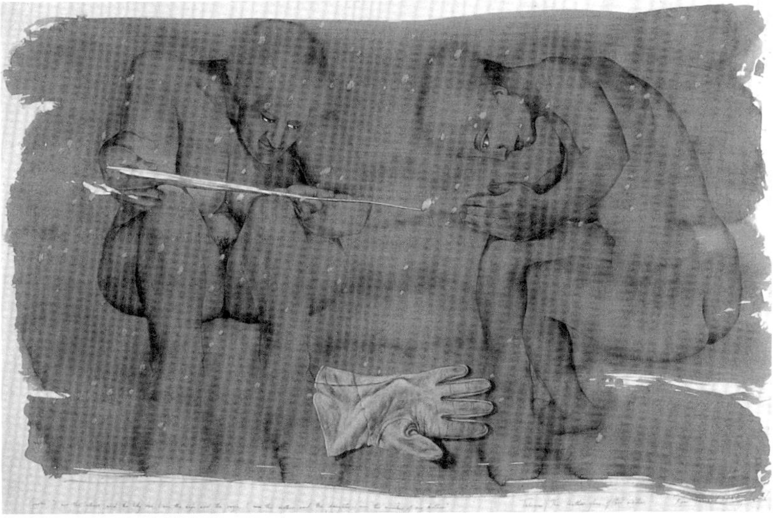

TALISMAN TEXT

I am the whore and the holy one.
I am the wife and the virgin.
I am the mother and the daughter.
I am the members of my mother.
Talisman, the leather glove of my mother.

I am the barren one
and many are her sons.
I am she whose wedding is great
and I have not taken a husband.
I am the midwife and she who does not bear.
I am the solace of my own labour pains.
Talisman, the wooden box from her father

I am the bride and the bridegroom
and it is my husband who begot me.
I am the mother of my father
and the sister of my husband
and he is my offspring.
Talisman, the embroidered shoe of a woman

I am the substance and the one who has no substance.
I am of the natures.
I am the silence that is incomprehensible
and the idea whose rememberance is frequent.
Talisman, the bronze mother and child from her parents

I am the voice whose sound is manifold
and the word whose appearance is multiple.
I am the utterance of my name.
Talisman, the seashell from her childhood

Give heed to my poverty and my wealth.
Do not be arrogant to me when I am cast out upon the earth
and you will find me in those that are to come.
And do not cast me out among those who are slain in violence.
For I, I am compassionate and I am cruel.
Talisman, the steel knife of her grandmother

In my weaknesses do not foresake me and do not be afraid
of my power.
For why do you despise my fear and curse my pride ?
Talisman, the wax doll from her childhood

I am she who exists in all fears
and I am the strength in trembling.
Talisman, the ceramic snake egg from herself

I am the one whom they call Life
and you have called Death.
I am the one whom they call Law
and you have called Lawlessness.
Talisman, the Mary Magdalene miniature from a stranger

I am the one whom you have scattered
and you have gathered me together.
Talisman, the opal necklace from her mother

I am control and the uncontrollable
I am the union and the dissolution
I am the abiding and the dissolving.
Talisman, the porcelain candlestick from her courtship

I prepare the bread and mind within.
I am the knowledge of my name.
I am the one who cries out, and I listen.
Talisman, the silver brooch from herself

Rose Garrard 1988
(Text derived from 'The Thunder, Perfect Mind' translated by George Macrae and Douglas Parrott, 'The Nag Hamadi Library in English', Bill Leiden 1977)

THE WAX DOLL FROM HER CHILDHOOD

Photograph
Louise Hallett Gallery

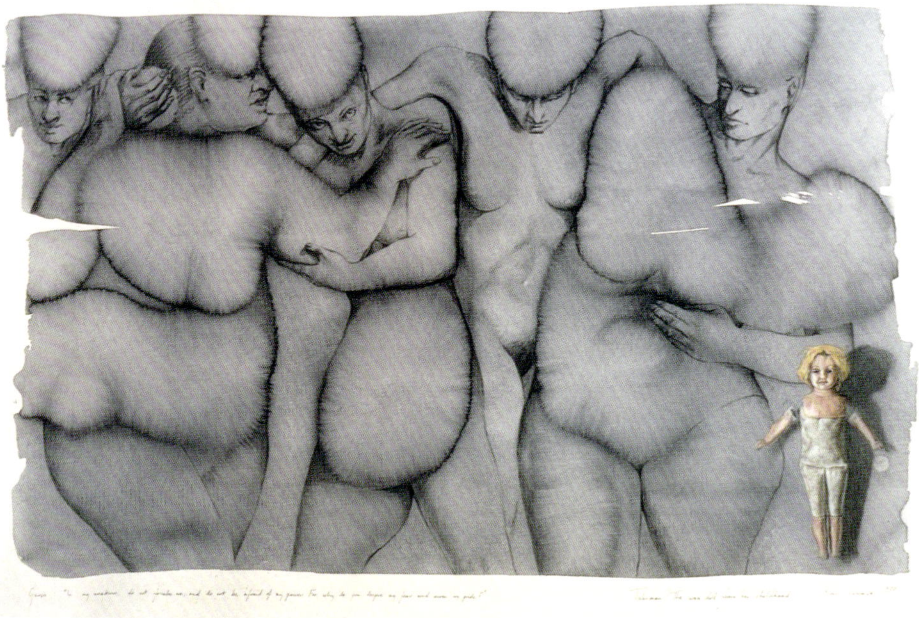

SITES

Louise Hallett Gallery London

Drumcroon Wigan Education Art Centre

COMPONENTS

Twelve monochrome drawings each containing one coloured, painted detail of an object belonging to the artist

COLLECTION

Victoria & Albert Museum London

Henry Moore Sculpture Trust for Leeds City Art Gallery and many private collectors.

Still from video
Fields and Frames
Productions

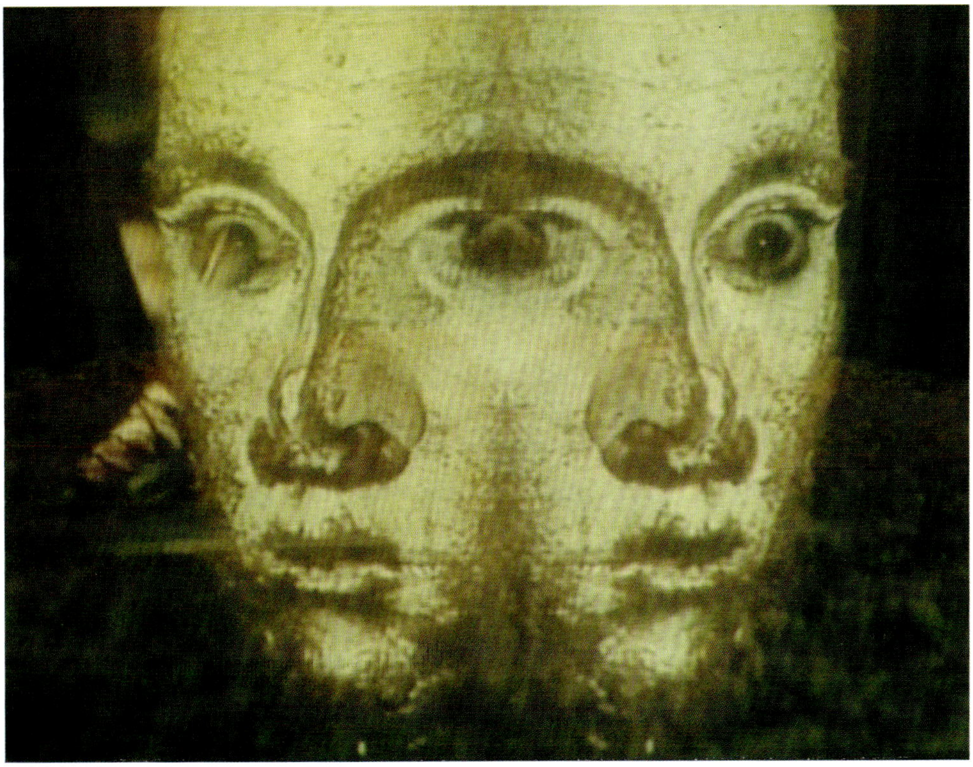

PRESS RELEASE Time as cyclical event where future directions are drawn from Celtic myths and emblems existing long ago. Faces as graven images, masks, confront the viewer inviting comparison with the living flesh of those today whose present begins with the past. The Celtic spirit flows with the seasons changes whose rhythms echo in the soundscore uniting traditional music and song with sounds from nature.

Tracing the nature of the 'Celt' through past mythology and imagery to present and future possibilities

Anna Ridley, Television Interventions, April 19 1990, Fields and Frames Productions, Channel 4

I am the dark spring running here
I am the wind on the water
the circles in the sacred spring
spinning the spiral of life
into the centre of the soul
I am a hawk on the cliff
I am a salmon in the pool
I am the strength of art
I am the source of the soul
I am the serpent of the stream, swimming,
the healer and the destroyer
resilient serpent
sensuous snake
interlacing signs into the mind's eye
into the sanctuary of the soul

'Celtic in Mind' sound track 1990 drawn from ancient Celtic texts

SITES

Broadcast nationally on Channel 4 Television and shown widely at Video Festivals both here and abroad

COMPONENTS

Four minute video tape combining original drawings, photographs using the Quantel Paintbox with live action and animation. Created and performed by the artist. Paintbox assistant Cavan Convery. Producer Anna Ridley, Series Producer Jane Rigby. A Fields and Frames Production. With thanks to Steve Partridge and Duncan of Jordanstone College of Art

COMMISSION

Channel 4 Television.

WHAT TURNS ME ABOUT HAS BEEN OVERCOME

Photograph
Nicola Percy

WHAT TURNS ME ABOUT HAS BEEN OVERCOME

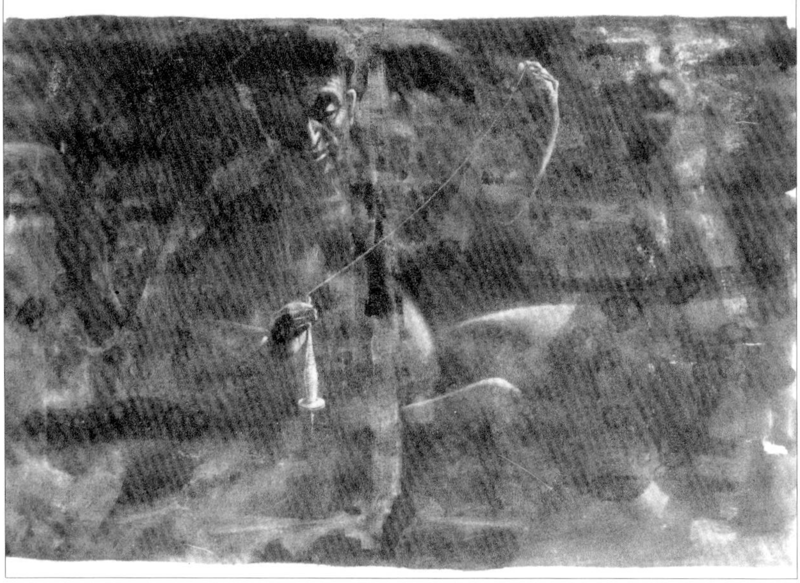

ARTIST'S NOTES Having stained the four large canvases with acrylic paint, I began to discern images which I developed by sanding away pigment with emery paper. In contrast to 'Talisman', where the images were arrived at by adding conte, the process in 'Journey Man' could be seen as a feminine one, arrived at by reductivist means, creating a negative in order to see a positive image.

Each of the four pieces is accompanied by a phrase of text presented above the canvases. These phrases form one sentence from another gnostic scroll, the 'Gospel of Mary', also discovered in 1946, in which Mary Magdalene reports her initial encounter with the risen Christ to the disbelieving disciples. The words are those of Jesus himself describing the process of his ascension through stages of questioning, and the replies made by his soul at different levels. Some of the original pages were used by the finder's mother to light her fire, before they were rescued, leaving intriguing gaps in his account.

What binds me has been slain,
What turns me about has been overcome,
My desire has been ended,
Ignorance has died.

While in the final stages of making these pieces I was visited by the friend who had originally given me the first gnostic text. After excitedly discussing the canvases with me he seemed very moved, but I couldn't quite understand the depth of his reaction. It came as a great shock three weeks later to be told that he had just died of Aids, and only the day before coming to see me had been diagnosed as HIV Positive. The images and texts remind me of our last conversation, but now I realise why his sense of identification with the piece was so powerful.

Rose Garrard 1994

SITE

'Shoemaker's Daughter' Air Gallery London

COMPONENTS

Four monochrome paintings on canvas with gnostic text from the Gospel of Mary on timber additions above.

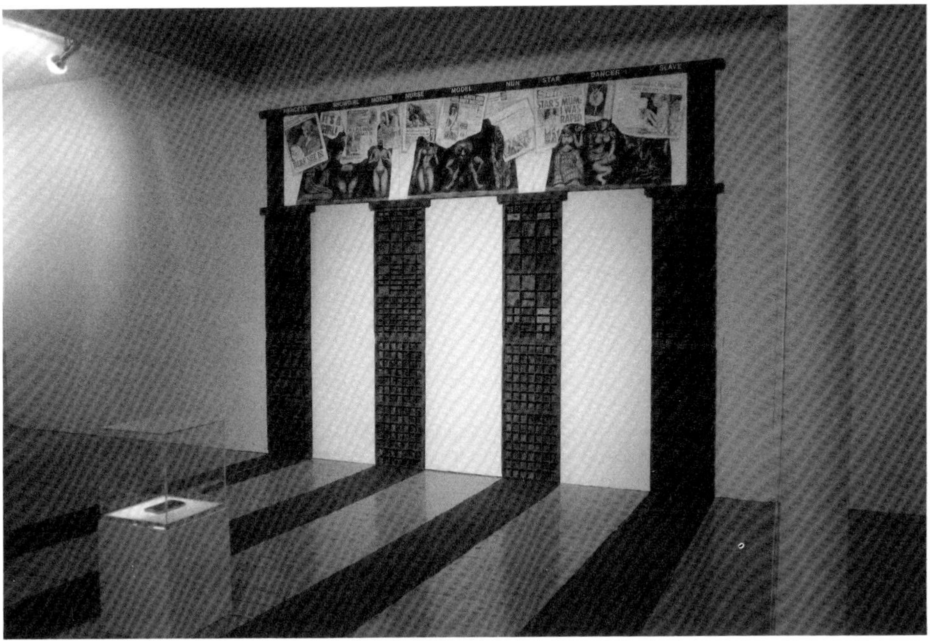

POPULAR PRESS While it is a shock to see the minuscule dimensions of a slipper made for the three inch foot of a Chinese noblewoman, foot binding nevertheless seems too archaic a symbol of female bondage to reflect the subtler forms of repression alive today.

Juxtaposed with the slippers is an image from a newspaper story of an eleven-year-old Asian girl busy at a sewing machine stitching shoes for her father's business. The implications of importing to Britain of third world customs like child labour or the imposition of purdah and the veil are far more pertinent than foot binding, and it's odd that Garrard focuses more on historical than the contemporary exploitation.

Sarah Kent, Time Out, November 23 1988

ARTIST'S NOTES Subtle and not so subtle forms of child labour have a long colonial tradition both here and abroad, and since the recession, are on the increase again in the poorest communities of Britain, regardless of their racial origin. The newspaper article about an Asian child working for her father in one of the many local East End sweat shops, stated she was actually making stiletto heeled ladies shoes. At its simplest, I was concerned in the piece to present a number of threads connecting the contemporary issues raised by this report, to the history of women and girl-children suffering in order to please men. There seems to me to be an obvious and direct parallel between 20th century western women wearing stilettos to feel attractive and 19th century eastern women wanting their feet bound for the same reason, the only change being that the power of the royal court to determine high fashion has been superseded by the power of the contemporary media.

The title 'Shoemaker's Daughter' implies this patriarchal inheritance, and is reinforced by the central presentation of a Victorian book 'How to Please'. The main images in the exhibition portray not only the child labour of the daughter in the current newspaper article, but other press images and texts which seek to disempower the independent roles which women do occupy today. These are shown literally covering over ancient female figures from all over the world, who represented these roles in a positive way within their cultures. Four embroidered women's shoes from a variety of continents and times were presented in small glass cases, the oldest of which was the tiny footbound shoe worn by an adult Chinese woman just over one hundred years ago. In this way the exhibition indicated the world-wide continuity of these systems of repression from the past to the present.

'Men took from you your ability to walk?' the Lord said incredulously, 'Is it the man who pulls the binding cloth to cripple a daughter's feet? No man could do a thing like that. No man could bear it.

'No man would marry a natural-footed woman. There is more to binding feet than just the binding ! ... Lady Guo Guo shook with fury and called after him.'

Rose Garrard 1994

(Text from 'A Visit from the Footbinder' by Emily Prager, Hogarth Press 1983)

SITE

'Shoemaker's Daughter' Air Gallery London

COMPONENTS

Two long painted canvas panels facing each other on opposite walls, supported by columns made of printers' block trays, linked by four felt strips. Four plinths and perspex cases each containing an embroidered shoe from various cultures. A fifth case containing a Victorian treatise entitled 'How to Please'.

LILITH; THE GOD EQUAL

Photograph
Nicola Percy

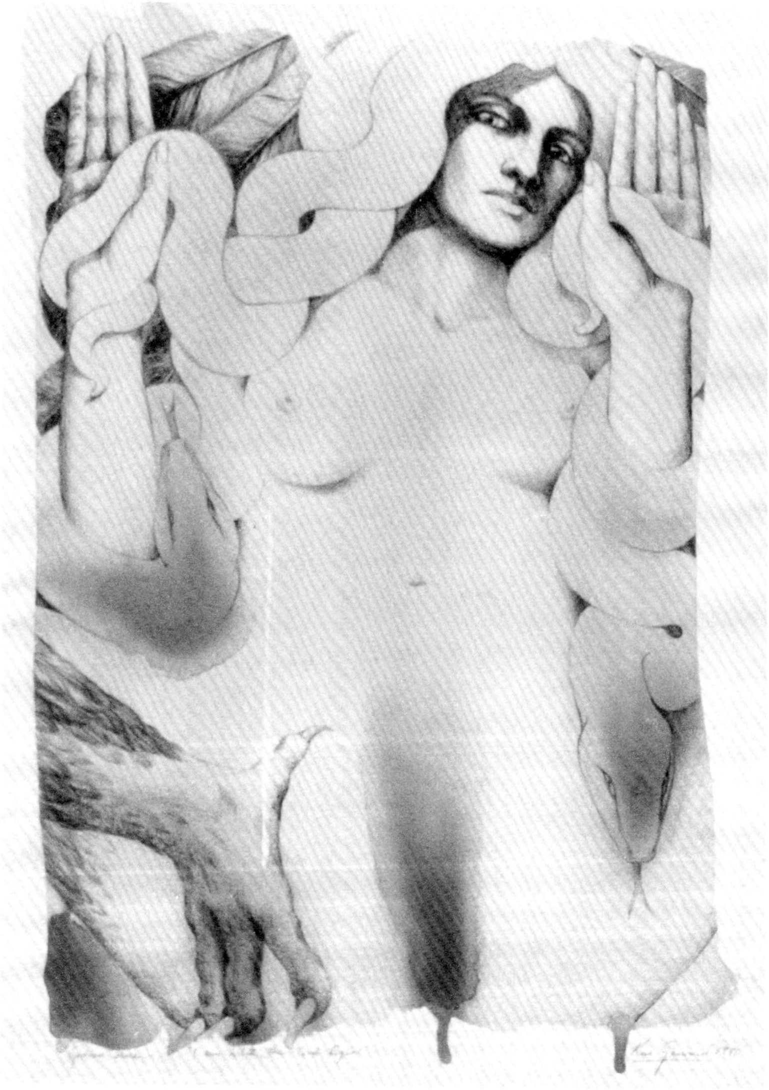

ARTIST'S NOTES Though I've always had an interest in ancient texts, stories and beliefs, after the accident my sudden awareness of the mortality of those close to me as well as myself, drew me into a closer, private search for my own relationship to spirituality. This enquiry surfaces most clearly but tentatively in public works such as the 'Talisman' series, 'Celtic in Mind' and 'Journey Man'.

Researching the 'goddess' figures for 'Shoemaker's Daughter' had rekindled my long term interest in ancient, positive representations of female god-heads and the Contemporary Art Society's invitation to make some new work for their art fair in Covent Garden focused me on re-presenting 'God-Birthers' from a wide range of cultures in this series of coloured drawings.

Rose Garrard 1994

SITE

Contemporary Art Society Art Fair Covent Garden London

COMPONENTS

Six single colour drawings on coloured acrylic washes in matching painted frames

COLLECTION

'Gaia, The God Bearer' Margot Messenger London

'Ashera, The God Birther' Roger and Cathy Wills Cheshire.

Photograph
Drumcroon Wigan

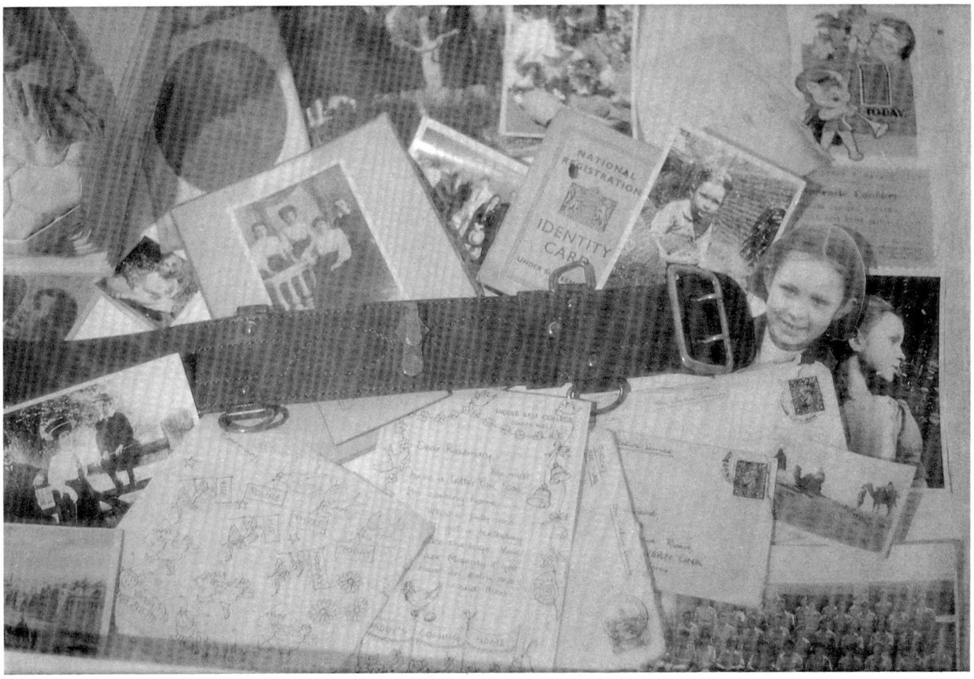

ART PRESS The Garrard household at this time was not a particularly happy place. She has vivid childhood memories of the 'persistent war' which raged between her parents and the ways in which she used her art to regain some respite from it. She recalls, 'I used it as a distraction for them because they both loved art but everything else was a problem. The one thing could do would be to draw either in front of them, or in another room, and then go and show it to them and every-thing else that was going on would stop; it was to input something positive as a way of getting some tranquility back into the house.'
Bryan Edmondson, 'Portrait of the Artist as a Woman' Drumcroon, Wigan 1991

ARTIST'S NOTES In this small room I concentrated all my framed childhood and adolescent drawings and paintings, returned to me after my mother's death in 1989, presenting them like wallpaper as part of 'Silences'. A glass case containing a 'progress book' of photos and other memorabilia focused the visitor on recorded parental expectations, a leather army belt suggested their oppressive behaviour, and a ticking clock measured the tension in the silence. Gallery staff attended training workshops in order that while working with visiting groups, they could then identify and discuss images by them, particularly children's images which might suggest that they had been battered or abused, giving out help-line numbers where appropriate.
Rose Garrard 1994

SITE

Drumcroon Wigan Education Art Centre

COMPONENTS

Glass case with family book, letters and other objects, including a leather army belt, 50 or 60 framed childhood and adolescent drawings and paintings.

Photograph
New Art Gallery
Calgary

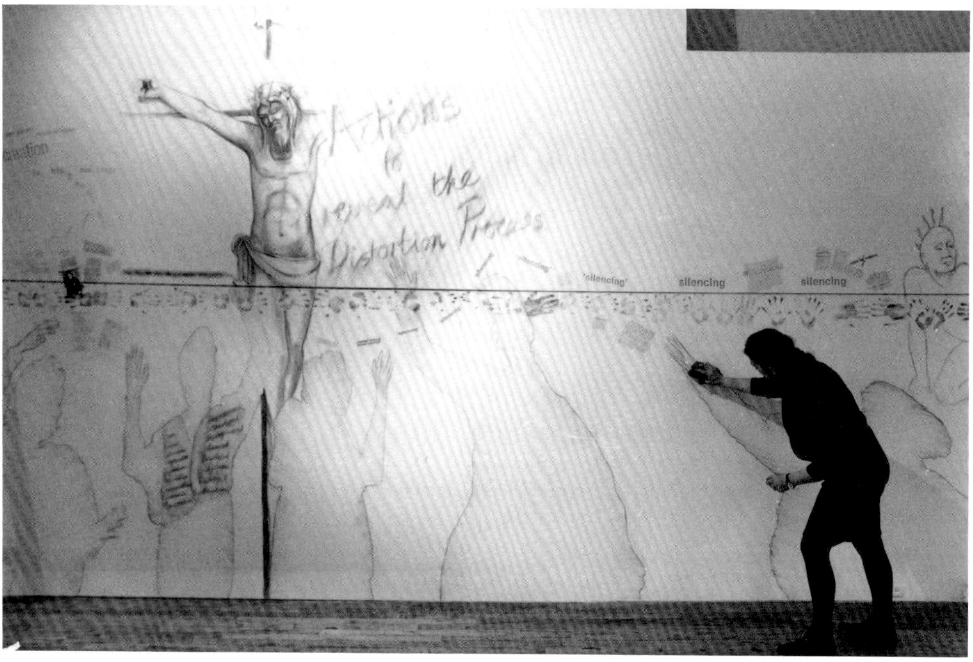

PRESS RELEASE Throughout the 1990's she has been engaged in a series of direct 'exchanges', searches for relationships between herself and the visitor in the process of making art, live in public. Garrard has been constructing 'arenas for conversation' with 'Calgary Conversation' 1991 and 'Disclosing Dialogues' 1992, which mark a new approach to artist's residencies as time-based live work.

Most mornings through an outreach programme which targets organisations and communities in the social context outside the art institution, Garrard goes to meet individuals and invites them to the gallery to talk with her as part of the work. The gallery installation develops in time as a 'conversation' between artist and individual visitor in which memories, texts, images and objects are contributed by them to guide Garrard's imaging process towards specific issues, people and events which visitors have experienced and regard as significant. Garrard in turn has installed a matrix of initial objects in the space which indicate clearly the subject around which the present dialogues are being focused. Each week is dedicated to examining an identified system of oppression, a process that is wholly dependent on participation by visitors who take an active and enthusiastic role, often returning frequently to see how the piece is developing.

Garrard sees her own ritual task as 'learning to listen to what's being said, not what I think I already know. A process of uncovering what I've learned not to see or hear. Creating a space for listening, for being surprised, for possibility, beyond my own prejudices and opinions.'

Bev Bytheway, Cornerhouse, Manchester 1993

Photograph
New Art Gallery
Calgary

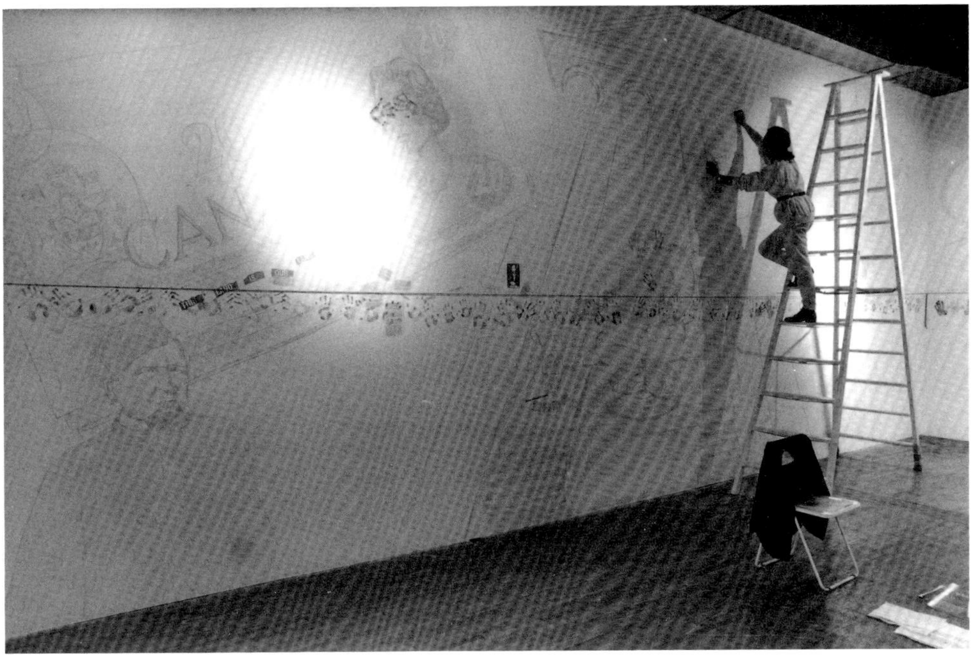

ARTIST'S NOTES I conceived these 'conversations' as beginning from the moment I stepped off the plane in Calgary. As a result a week later the gallery contained a central installation which summarised my colonial preconceptions of Canada; eight portrait drawings of indigenous Canadians taken from photographs by 19th century western settlers and a logged tree hung upside down above a reflective pool of dark car oil. In tiny gold frames single words summarised the processes by which peoples throughout the world are subjugated. The gallery itself ran from north to south and I dedicated each of its walls to an exploration of a system of oppression; Paternalism,Colonialism, Imperialism and Racism – which during the first week of my 'research' had emerged as perhaps the most cared about but least discussed issues effecting the people of Calgary.

As a daily live process throughout the three weeks, 'in conversation' with the feelings, experiences and information shared with me by visitors, I drew a single colour 'mural' in conté on each of the walls. These 'murals' were, in sequence, black, red, yellow and white, the colours which indigenous Canadians identify with each racial group in the world. Whilst working with each colour I wore clothing of the same colour. Every actual conversation was focused primarily around the single system of oppression that I was then engaged in drawing, creating a multi-faceted picture of the experiences of people from many racial origins during the process of becoming Canadian.

'One of the first things is for people to engage in dialogue together, without trying to solve any problem. That would certainly change culture and society. What we need is to be able to talk, to communicate. At present there are great differences and many of these are not negotiable. What is needed is a dialogue in the real sense of the word 'dialogue', which means 'flowing through'. The basic idea of this dialogue is to be able to talk, while suspending your opinions, holding them in front of you, while neither suppressing them nor insisting upon them. Not trying to convince but simply to understand. The first thing is that we must perceive the whole meaning of everybody, without having to say who's right and who's wrong. It is more important that we all see the same thing. That will create a new frame of mind in which there is a common consciousness.'

Rose Garrard 1991

(Text from David Bohm, Quantum Physicist, 1990, 'Art Science and Spirituality' Academy Editions, London 1990)

Photograph
New Art Gallery
Calgary

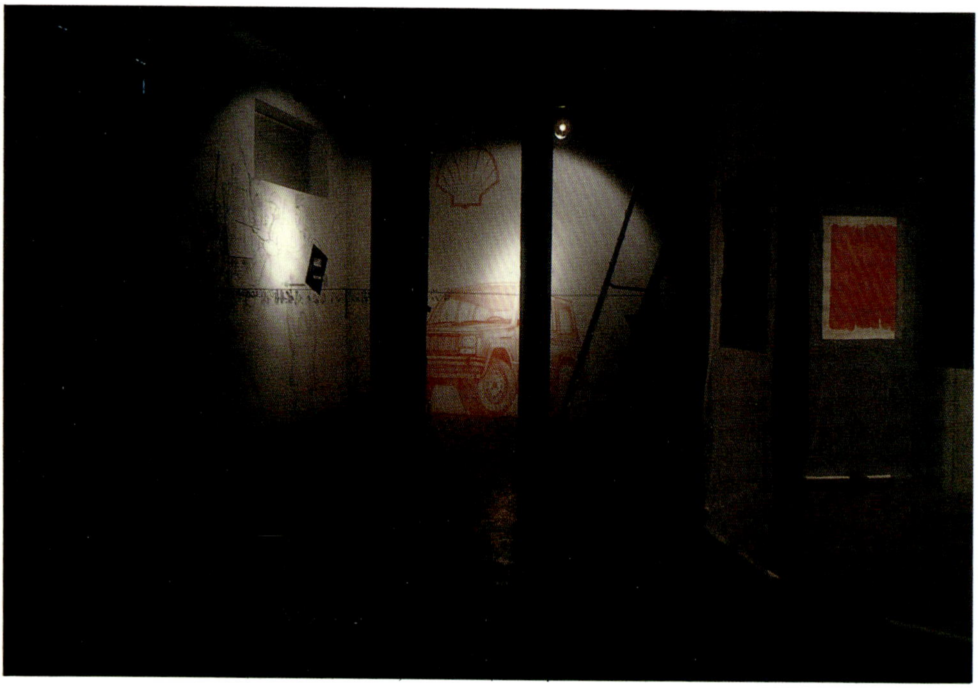

ARTIST'S NOTES The issues most often brought up were the rights of native Canadians, particularly their land rights, as following recent confrontations such as that with the National Guard at Okha, everyone was concerned that the violence shouldn't escalate. A dispute over the building of the 'Old Man Dam' across a river on the nearby Peigan Reservation had led to gun shots, arrests and a local trial which continued for most of my stay. This context informed the individual contributions made by people, and consequently the imaging process, and was responded to in a direct way by Shirley Bear a native Canadian, artist and political rights activist, who I first met at Banff Arts Centre.

I had begun work on the third wall – Imperialism (Yellow) – and was drawing a huge 20 dollar note with a fairly meticulous likeness of the Queen's head on it, when Shirley came in. She rigorously questioned what I was doing, and then told me the first origins of her anger at this image which so offended her. This was when as a child she had been made to wait for hours in the freezing cold as one of the 'Indians' placed on the route of the Queen's Royal Tour of Canada. Then she had only caught a glimpse of the Queen, but now she had determined a rather different relationship. Shirley questioned how shared my drawing process really was, and if she could participate in it. She slowly climbed the ladder and placing her hands over the eyes of the image, made two black handprints in a ritual of exorcism.

Following every exchange, I had been inviting each individual to contribute their hand-prints to the wall, as an act of continuity and mark of participation rather than agreement. Nobody refused, and no-one but Shirley felt they had sufficient reason to justify deviating from this line.

These hand-prints eventually formed a continuous row around the gallery linking issues and events contributed by disparate voices in the community. These included local people who were waitresses, shop assistants, feminists, Jehovah's Witnesses, Catholics, racists, native rights activists, artists, writers, Vietnamese refugees, cowboys, European immigrants, settlers, indigenous Canadians and tourists. Perhaps because of the public face of 'political correctness' in Canada, many people seemed relieved to talk through their opinions and experiences in a non-judgemental way, on a one to one basis, sometimes realising for the first time how extreme their views and feelings were. All visitors were encouraged to return and bring an object image or text which related to our discussion. Some came back again and again to contribute these and support the development of the piece.

Rose Garrard 1994

SITE

New Art Gallery Calgary Canada

COMPONENTS

Twelve foot high felled tree, four foot circular metal dish of engine-oil, eight monochrome portraits supported on gauze hangings, twelve tiny gilt frames with text, four chairs, objects given by visitors, four plain walls each with a single colour conté mural, texts and visitors hand prints. Artist as performer wearing 1. black 2. red 3. yellow and 4. white clothing. Artists residency of four weeks duration

COMMISSION

The Canada Council.

Photograph
Vancouver Art Gallery

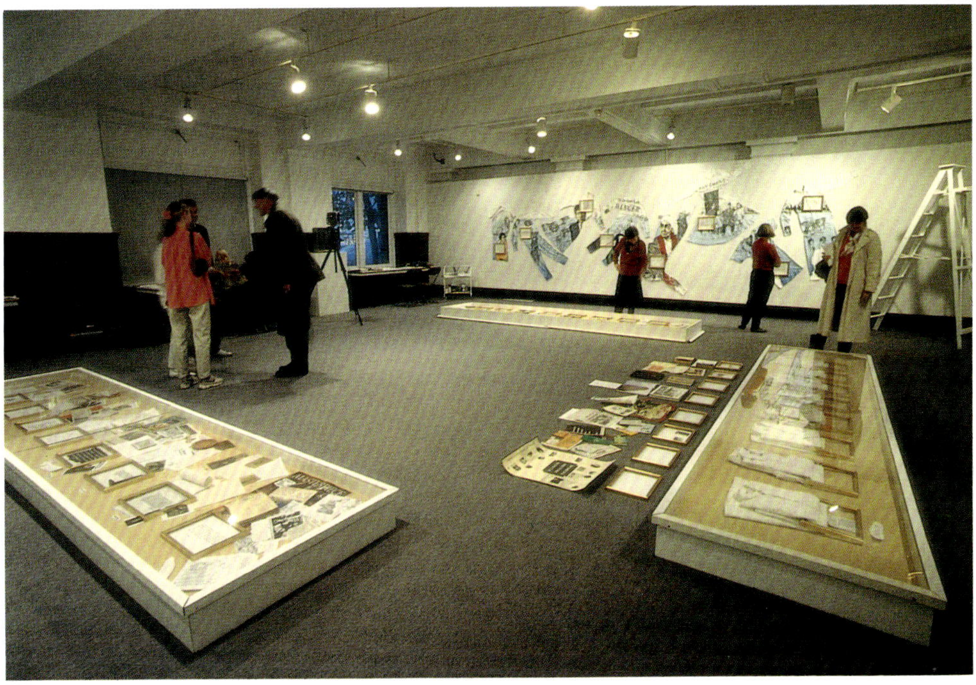

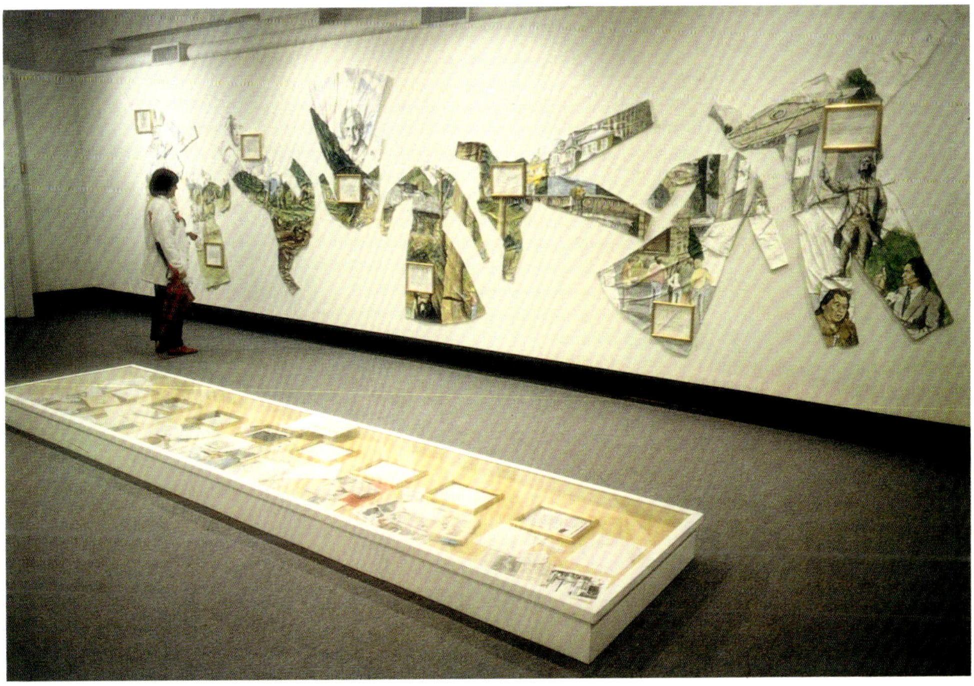

Photograph
Vancouver Art Gallery

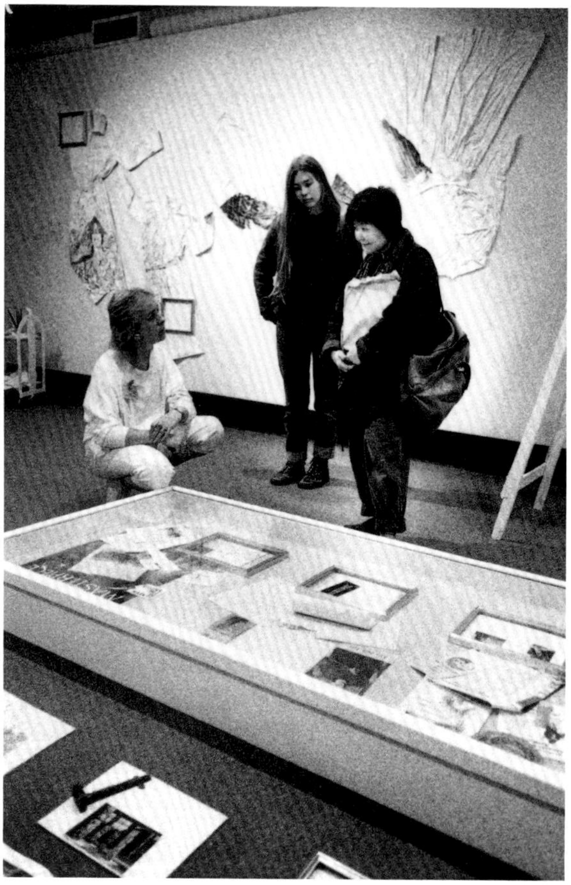

ART PRESS Garrard's career has centred on the use of her talents and skills as a painter and sculptress as tools for process-based performance art. Her body and intelligence is at the centre of the work as are those of the viewer-participants. The work, the art, is about human interactions. At the point of display, usually our first point of contact with works of art, Garrard's work is dormant; in hibernation, so to speak, awaiting continuation. It constitutes a record of where we have been, the roads not taken, and always, the possibilities of going on. The empty wall, exhibition cases, frames and folded clothes form a tabula rasa, evoking memory, history, the present and the future as much as the picturing, the objects and documentation do.

Rose Garrard describes this work as 'a process-based, live work of three weeks duration.' It began, as other projects have begun in other galleries such as Birmingham City Museum and Art Gallery and the New Art Gallery in Calgary, with 'a central conversation piece', a stimulus for the discussions to begin, consisting of props and artifacts. In this case, the material forming the 'conversation piece' was three, large exhibition cases, resting on the floor of the gallery, filled with a multitude of folded, white, used clothes, gathered from Vancouver's thrift shops, and small, 8 x 11in, gilded, wooden picture frames. A few objects appeared in the first case. These were images from the previous work in Calgary and a group of archival documents from the gallery's collection – letters and photos of Emily Carr and her parents – as well as reproductions of some of Carr's works. In the centre of the room there were two sets of clothing, arranged and primed to be used as the support for painting. On the wall hung a number of these 'canvases', each containing one of the gold frames, ready for the picturing to begin.

In preparation for her visit, a number of gallery staff and volunteers were involved in 'preparing the ground' for Rose's activity. Brainstorming together, we developed a list of individuals and organizations engaged in many sectors of Canadian life. Some of them were advocates or advocacy groups, some service or research organizations; some were government agencies for elected officials, some might be perceived as disenfranchised, by choice or circumstance, from social processes. Letters were sent and telephone calls made to discuss the issues which concerned then and to invite them to visit Rose and to enter into the development of the work in the gallery. When she arrived, the banner of invitation to the public went up on the Robson Street entrance. And wherever she spoke and to whomever, on buying excursions or at public lectures, the invitation was extended to participate in the project by visiting and talking with her at the gallery.

Garrard's performance is, in her view, a transformative position, reclaiming social processes. 'It's about hearing' she says, 'not about reaching agreement'. For Garrard, the conversations are central to the work, but the activity of making creates the opportunity and the stimulus for the conversations. Visitors do not gather to witness the artist. Witnessing, on everyone's part, stimulates the creation of her work.

Photograph
Vancouver Art Gallery

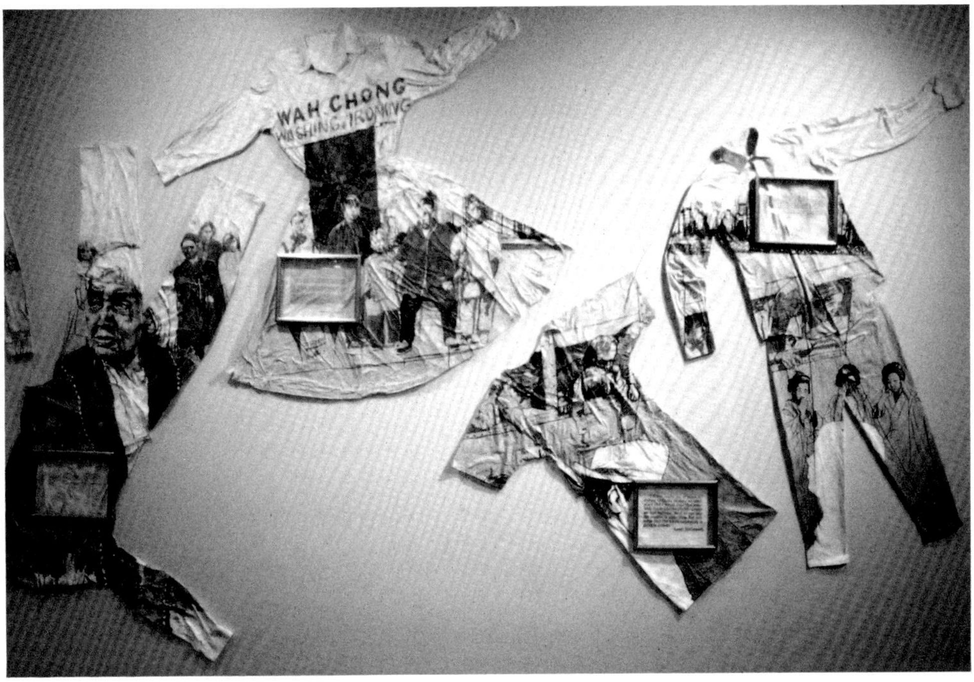

The month of October proved to be a monumental one for Canadians. During the time of Garrard's visit, we were engaged in the constitutional debates surrounding the Charlotte town Accord and, finally, in the referendum which resulted in rejection of the Accord by 'the people of Canada', as the politicians and the media love to call us. In the midst of the measured yet heated debates, we Canadians sought to illuminate our confusion about the many, varied issues of our lurching, emerging notion of our own nationhood. Garrard's first wall, on the subject of paternalism, reflected these discussions. It began with references to her position as a British artist in our midst, the latest in a long line of paternalistic, colonizing eyes turned on this place and its peoples.

Gazing at this part of the piece, a fractured mural, one is struck by the overwhelming images of the landscape which dominate, as ever, the new arrival to Canada's West Coast. Whatever the conversations might have been between the artist and the visitors, the work mirrors back to us a number of concerns: the relationship between European colonizers and the indigenous peoples of the First Nations; the paradoxes of economic development which produce one of the highest rates of homelessness; the place of women within the patriarchal structures of Canadian society, and the relations of political power which emerged during the constitutional debates. In and amongst these contemporary threads were laced historical references to icons of this place such as the monument of Captain George Vancouver, Emily Carr (Canada's most famous woman artist) and the gallery itself. But unlike the television coverage which we dutifully tuned into every evening, Garrard's representations provided us with a rich tapestry of images drawn from very individual personal stories through which to contemplate the complexities of our situation here. In the exhibition cases, information, documentation, newspaper articles, quotes from her visitors, and books, photos and objects contributed by them add to the richness of our contemplation.

During the final week of her residency, Garrard, began painting on the opposite wall, investigating the subject of racism in this place. Here one confronted a seascape of faces, of many different ancestries, from many moments, past and present, during which we have been involved in negotiating our social contract.

Tonight, in the dark, our experiences in this room – the conversations, the ghostly canvases of clothing once worn by people living in Vancouver and the images representing our shared time together during this month – cloud into memories. Only the work remains as a trace of history to mark the fact that we were here, then.

Judith Mastai, Vancouver Art Gallery, October 1992

SITE

Vancouver Art Gallery Canada

COMPONENTS

Twenty-four, white, male and female outfits of clothes, sixteen of them primed and acrylic painted during three weeks of live, task based activity. Forty eight A4 gold frames. Two twelve foot long museum display cases, gradually filled with objects given by visitors. The third glass case remained filled with eight neatly folded sets of white clothes each with a small gold frame labelled 'Colonialism' Artist as performer in white clothing. Artists residency of four weeks duration.

COMMISSION

Vancouver Art Gallery Canada.

PRESS RELEASE Rose Garrard will be working live in the Gallery as part of her artist's residency at Cornerhouse from 22 March 1994. Her work will be based on a similar process to her recent pieces in Art Galleries at Calgary and Vancouver, Canada beginning with an 'arena for conversation' an initial site specific installation in which she will talk with individual members of the public. For three weeks these exchanges will guide the direction of her image making, charting the further development of the installation in the space.

Conversations will be focused around the visitor's own experience of systems of oppression – paternalism, colonialism, racism – and from these the artist will create visual images which are relevant to both the particular social context of Manchester and the world concerns facing us today. This process is entirely dependent on exchanges with visitors. Our thoughts, beliefs and experiences expressed in one to one conversations with the artist, and subsequently related texts, images and objects which people may lend or contribute to the piece, will shape and focus Garrard's continuous drawing and painting activity in the Gallery.

During the mornings she will also undertake a series of outreach activities, including meetings with people who are key members of groups, communities and organisations within Manchester, inviting them to come as individuals and talk with her in the Gallery as part of the work. Through these exchanges with visitors in the space itself, Garrard will research the public and private concerns of people in the city, what we care about on a personal, social and cultural level, and what actions we can take now to bring a more optimistic future into existence.

Bev Bytheway, Cornerhouse, Manchester, March 1994

EDUCATION AND TRAINING

1965-66 Stourbridge College of Art, West Midlands
Foundation Course in Art & Design
1966-69 Birmingham College of Art
1st Class Honours Degree in Sculpture (Dip. A.D.)
1969-1970 Chelsea School of Art, Post Graduate M.A.
(Higher Diploma in Sculpture)
1970-71 Ecole de Beaux Arts, Paris
Scholarship from the British Council/French Government

AWARDS AND RESIDENCIES

1969 Multiples International Prize, judged by Eduardo Paolozzi
Museum of Modern Art, Oxford
1971 Prix D'Honneur De Paris for Sculpture
International Art Exhibition of Scholarship Holders
ORTF Centre, Paris
1979 Arts Council of Great Britain
Purchase Award for Performance Surveillance, ACGB Collection
1981 Greater London Arts Association, Major Award
1982 Whitechapel Art Gallery Artists in Schools Residency funded by GLAA,
Central Foundation School for Girls, Bow, London
1983 Birmingham City Museum & Art Gallery, Artist in Residence in collaboration with Ikon Gallery
1991 The New Art Gallery, Calgary, Alberta, Canada
Artist in Residence, British & Canada Councils
1992 Vancouver Art Gallery, Canada, Artist in Residence
British Council

SOLO EXHIBITIONS

1992 Disclosing Dialogues
live-art residency
Vancouver Art Gallery, Canada
1991 Calgary Conversation
live-art residency
New Art Gallery, Calgary, Canada
Portrait of the Artist as a Woman
Drumcroon, Wigan Education Art Centre
1988 Talisman
Louise Hallett Gallery, London
Shoemaker's Daughter
Air Gallery, London
Out of Line
Edge 88
London & Newcastle Upon Tyne
1987 Redressing the Balance
Neue Gesellschaft fur bildende Kunst
West Berlin, Germany
Casting Room Two
Cornerhouse, Manchester
1986 Casting Room One
Third Generation of Women Sculptors
Canterbury Festival
1985 Openings
Laing Art Gallery, Newcastle upon Tyne
Tumbled Frame
ICA, London
1984 Between Ourselves
Ikon Gallery, Birmingham & touring to
Bluecoat Gallery, Liverpool
Rochdale Art Gallery
Midland Group, Nottingham
Arnolfini, Bristol
South Hill Park, Bracknell
ICA, London
1983 Frames of Mind
Kettle's Yard, Cambridge
Frameworks
Lewis Johnstone Gallery, London
1982 The Fall, Women Live
Arnolfini, Bristol
1980 Surveillance
International Performance Symposium
Lyon, France
1977 Incidents in a Garden
Acme Gallery, London

GROUP EXHIBITIONS

1992 Womens Art at New Hall College
Cambridge University
Traces of the Figure
Stoke-on-Trent City Museum and Art Gallery
and touring to Cartwright Hall, Bradford
1991 Women's Video Festival
Dortmund, Germany
Video Festival
Heuroville, France
1990 Contemporary Art Society Art Fair
Covent Garden, London
Television Interventions
Third Eye Centre, Glasgow
1989 Images of Women
Leeds City Art Gallery
Picturing People
British Council Touring Exhibition
Kuala Lumpur
1988 20th Century Drawings
Birmingham City Museum & Art Gallery
Object and Image, British Art in the 1980s
Stoke-on-Trent City Museum and Art Gallery
Something Solid
Cornerhouse, Manchester
1987 Confrontations, The Role of Controversy in Art
Laing Art Gallery, Newcastle upon Tyne
and touring to
Cornerhouse, Manchester
Cartwright Hall, Bradford
Heroes
Air Gallery, London
Art in Action
Dartington, Spacex & Plymouth Art Centres
Self Portraits
Artsite, Bath & nationwide tour
Hong Kong International Film Festival
1986 Living Art
Guinness Hop Store, Dublin
Dadarama
Riverside Studios, London
Three Sisters
National Garden Festival
Stoke-on-Trent
Video Start

Bologna, Italy
World Wide Video Festival
The Hague, Holland
The Golden Thread
Harris Museum and Art Gallery, Preston
Conceptual Clothing
Ikon Gallery, Birmingham & touring
1985 Australian Biennale
Sydney, Perth, Brisbane and Melbourne
Kunst mit Eigen-Sinn
Museum des 20 Jahrhunderts, Vienna
Whitechapel Open
Whitechapel Art Gallery, London
Human Interest
Cornerhouse, Manchester
1984 Locarno Video Festival
Switzerland
Aperto
Venice Biennale
Guns
Interim Art, London
Cross Currents
Royal College of Art, London
Video 84
Montreal, Canada
Film and Video Festival
Los Angeles, California
Recent British Video
ICA, London &
Toronto, Canada
Art Within Reach
Air Gallery, London
Self Expressed
Spacex Gallery, Exeter
1983 New Art
Tate Gallery, London
International Contemporary Art Fair
Barbican Arts Centre, London
Faces
Monica Kinley Gallery, London
Gallery Artists
Lewis Johnstone Gallery, London
Whitechapel Open
Whitechapel Art Gallery, London
1982 Live to Air
Tate Gallery, London
Women Live
Basement Group, Newcastle upon Tyne
1981 Plastic work by Performance Artists
ELAC, Lyon, France
1980 About Time
ICA, London & touring to
Arnolfini, Bristol
Third Eye Centre, Glasgow
Nuclear Disarmament
Acme Gallery, London
1979 Lives
Arts Council Purchase Exhibition
Serpentine Gallery, London & touring
1978 Hayward Annual
South Bank Centre, London
1977 Art for Society
Whitechapel Art Gallery, London
1975 Design in Performance
Portman Gallery, London
1974 Body Box
Victoria & Albert Museum, London
1971 London Now
Messenhallen, West Berlin
Artistes Etrangers
ORTF Centre, Paris
Spectrum
Alexandra Palace, London
Triangle
Congress Hall, London
1970 First Show
Serpentine Gallery, London
City of London Festival
St Paul's Cathedral Square, London
Summer Summary
Alwin Gallery, London

PUBLIC COLLECTIONS

Arts Council of Great Britain
Birmingham City Museum & Art Gallery
Contemporary Art Society
Henry Moore Sculpture Trust
Leeds City Art Gallery
Victoria & Albert Museum

PRIVATE AND CORPORATE COLLECTIONS

Alwin Gallery
Angela Flowers Gallery
L.E.B. Transport
Lewis Johnstone Gallery
Lloyds Bank Ltd
Raymond J. Cecil & Partners
Walter Thompson & Co Ltd
and many private collections

TELEVISION COVERAGE

1990 Celtic in Mind Channel 4 Commission
Artists works for television to celebrate Glasgow 1990
Fields and Frames Productions
1988 Self Portraits
90-minute HTV documentary on exhibition featuring five artists
Out of Line short feature by Thames TV News
1987 Celebration 30-minute documentary on Garden Festival
Stoke-on-Trent by Central Television
1986 Tumbled Frame broadcast on Dutch Cable TV to 40,000 homes
1985 Kunsthonia cultural journal programme on Channel 2 German TV, review of Berlin retrospective
Imaginary Women Channel 4 60-minute documentary
Six creative women in discussion (Toyah Wilcox, Katherine Hamnett, Susan Hiller, Helen Chadwick, Gaby Agis, Rose Garrard) with Marina Warner, produced by Gina Newsome
Review on Tyne Tees Television
Tumbled Frame Channel 4 Commission
Dadarama series of Artists works for Television. Annalogue TV Productions Ltd. 25 minutes

TELEVISION COVERAGE

1984 Between Ourselves BBC North Oxford Roadshow 7-minute documentary
1983 Pandora the Bringer of Gifts Television South West Commission for series A Private View, 20 minutes
1980 Arena BBC 1 documentary on women artists
1977 A Day in the Garden BBC 2 documentary featuring Incidents in a Garden
1974 Body Box, Victoria & Albert Museum, documented by Spanish Television featuring Universal Man
Central Office of Information Documentary on same exhibition as above
1970 Several short items on News and Arts Magazine programmes for BBC & ITV showing sculptures at the Serpentine Gallery and outside St Pauls Cathedral

ARTIST'S CATALOGUES

1991 Portrait of the Artist as a Woman
Drumcroon, Wigan Education Art Centre
1988 Talisman
Louise Hallett Gallery, London
1987 Rose Garrard
Neue Gesellschaft fur bildende Kunst, West Berlin
Catalogue essay by Marina Warner
1984 Between Ourselves
Ikon Gallery, Birmingham
Catalogue essay by John Roberts and artist interviewed by Sue Arrowsmith

GROUP CATALOGUES

1990 Television Interventions 19.4.90
Fields and Frames Productions for Channel 4
1989 Images of Women
Leeds City Art Gallery
1988 Edge 88: Biennale of Experimental Art
Something Solid
Cornerhouse, Manchester
1987 British Art in the 20th Century
Royal Academy, London
1986 Conceptual Clothing
Ikon Gallery, Birmingham
The Golden Thread
Harris Museum and Art Gallery, Preston
World Wide Video Festival by Eric Daans
De Dageraad, Holland
1985 Human Interest
Cornerhouse, Manchester
Kunst mit Eigen-Sinn
Locker Verlag, Vienna & Munich
Living Art
Orchard Press, Ireland
1984 The Venice Biennale 84
Electra, Milano
British Canadian Video Exchange
Canada House, London
Cross Currents
Royal College of Art, London
Self Expressed
Plymouth Arts Centre
1983 New Art
Tate Gallery, London
1981 Symposium International D'Art Performance
Hubert Besascier, Lyon, France
1980 About Time
ICA, London
1979 Lives by Derek Boshier
Arts Council of Great Britain
1978 Hayward Annual 78
Arts Council of Great Britain

SELECTED PUBLICATIONS: BOOKS & SOME MAJOR ARTICLES

1991 21 Was Nun?
Neue Gesellschaft fur bildende Kunst, Berlin
1990 Future Tense New Art for the Nineties
Robert Hewison, Methuen
1989 Picturing People – British Figurative Arts
Norbert Lynton, British Council
1988 Monuments and Maidens
Marina Warner, published by Wiedenfeld and Nicholson
Framing Feminism
Griselda Pollock and Rozsika Parker, Pandora Press
1987 The Self Portrait – A Modern View
Edward Lucie-Smith, Sarena Press
2D / 3D Where do we go from here?
Conference Papers, Newcastle Upon Tyne Polytechnic
Visibly Female, Feminism and Art Today
Hilary Robinson, Camden Press
1985 Freibeuter No 24 – Die Kunsterlin Rose Garrard
Barbara Beck and Beatrice Stammer, Klaus Wagenbach Germany
Women's Images of Men
Sarah Kent & Jacqueline Morreau, Writers & Readers
1983 Cinq Ans D'Art Performance
Comportement-Environment-Performance, Lyon, France

EXAMINING EXPERIENCE: B.A. FINE ART (UNLESS OTHERWISE STATED)

1978-79 Internal Assessor, Reading University, all media
1981-85 External, Trent Polytechnic, multi-media
1982 External, Byam Shaw School of Art, 3rd Area College Certificate
1983-86 External, Middlesex Polytechnic, time-based
1983-87 External, Slade School of Art, sculpture
1984 External, Central School of Art, sculpture
1985 External, Leeds Polytechnic, 3rd Area
1985 External, Byam Shaw School of Art, sculpture and 3rd Area, College Certificate
1986 External, Royal College of Art, multi-media
1986-89 External, Preston Polytechnic, time-based
1986-90 External, University of Ulster at Belfast, M.A. sculpture, multi-media and performance
1986-92 Internal, Dartington College of Art, all media B.A. Art and Social Context

LECTURING, REGULAR PART-TIME

1971-75 United States International University, sculpture
1972-78 Mary Ward Centre Euston, Head of Sculpture A.E.
1976-80 Reading University, Time-based studies, B.A. & M.A.
1977-82 Epson School of Art, Foundation, all subjects
1979-81 Trent Polytechnic, sculpture and multi-media B.A.
1980-86 Sheffield Polytechnic, Communication Arts B.A.
1981-84 Croydon College of Art, Video & T.V., College Certificate
1984-92 Dartington College of Arts, Art and Social Context B.A. and Visual Performance B.A.

Public and Visiting Lecturing

At numerous Universities, Polytechnics and Colleges of Art throughout Britain including: Belfast, Birmingham, Brighton, Byam Shaw, Canterbury, Chelsea, Glasgow, Goldsmiths, Leeds, Maidstone, Newcastle, Portsmouth, Royal College of Art, St Martins, Sheffield, Slade.

Abroad: Dublin University Ireland, Vancouver and Calgary Art Schools Canada.

Also at many Art Galleries and Museums including Arnolfini Bristol, Birmingham City Museum and Art Gallery, Cornerhouse Manchester, ICA London, Ikon Gallery Birmingham, Kettle's Yard Cambridge, Leeds City Art Gallery, National Gallery London, Tate Gallery Liverpool.

Organisational Experience

1976-77 Selection Panel
Acme Gallery, London
1980 Selection Panel New Contemporaries
1979-81 Selector and organiser About Time
ICA, London
1981-82 Awards panel, Greater London Arts Association
1981 External Awards Judge, South West Arts
1983-84 Purchaser for the ACGB
1983 Selection Panel New Contemporaries
1984-85 Curator of the British section for Kunst mit Eigen-Sinn
Museum des 20 Jahrhunderts, Vienna
1984-87 Art Panel member
Council for National Academic Awards
1984-89 Visual Arts Panel member
South West Arts Association
1985 Selector Whitechapel Open
Whitechapel Art Gallery, London
1987 Curator and organiser Art in Action
Dartington, Spacex and Plymouth Arts Centres
1987-89 Arts Panel member, ACGB
1989-92 Live Art Advisory Group, ACGB
1990-91 Curator and organiser Art for Amnesty auction for Amnesty International

Other Experience

1969-1989 Freelance Designer, Props and Model maker to BBC, Theatres, Magazines and Advertising. Including work in special effects models, animation puppets, scenic design and manufacture 3D caricature, costumes, monumental and miniature sculpture, robots, scale models, 2D/3D portraits, illustration and props in a wide range of scale and media.

Work on programmes for BBC include: Verdi's Macbeth props scenery and costume accessories, Dr Who sets and costumes including Voc Robots, Pinocchio scale models, Grace Jones special masks, Top of the Pops props/scenery, Barbara in the House of Grebe portrait sculpture, Valley of the Kings props, It's Not the Nine O'Clock News, Spitting Image, Lenny and Jerry Spectacular chroma-key models, Little and Large, Frog Across the Andes sculpture, Hansel and Gretel landscape models, and other Drama and Light Entertainment programmes.

1971-74 Arts Consultant to Architects advising on improving existing schemes such as Liverpool Shopping Precinct and Elephant and Castle Shopping Centre, resulting in numerous commissions, including 'The Spirit of the City' a 30ft high bronze wall sculpture near Old Street Tube. At that time this was the largest bronze erected in London since the war.

Rose Garrard wishes to thank

Anna Ridley
Andre Von Graan
Judith Mastai
Louisa Buck
Nicola Percy
Pauleen Morphett
Cathy and Roger Wills
Michael Kipriano
Jane Ilari
Don Holtum
Bo Carter
Sacha Brent
Andrew Brown
Shirley Chan
Shirley Bear
Margaret Anderson
Arthur Lang
Sandra Tivey and Nelson
Vivien Lovall
Jeni Walwin
Anne Bean
Peter Silverleaf
Paul Johnstone
Jonathan Harvey and Rita Harris
Jon Bewley
Bev Bytheway

and many others too numerous to mention without whom the work would not have been possible